THE
HORSERACING
FORMULA

**PROVEN BETTING FORMULAS FOR
WINNING MONEY AT THE TRACK!**

THE HORSERACING FORMULA

PROVEN BETTING FORMULAS FOR WINNING MONEY AT THE TRACK!

WALTER GIBSON

GBC PRESS
P. O. Box 98115
Las Vegas, NV 89193
www.gamblersbookclub.com

GBC Press books are published by Gambler's Books Club in Las Vegas, Nevada. Since 1964, the legendary GBC has been the reigning authority on gambling publications and the only dedicated gambling bookstore anywhere.

Library of Congress Catalog Number: 2011925833
ISBN 10: 1-58042-285-3   ISBN 13: 978-1-58042-285-7
GBC Press is an imprint of Cardoza Publishing

GBC PRESS
c/o Cardoza Publishing
P.O. Box 98115, Las Vegas, NV 89193
Toll-Free Phone (800)522-1777
email: info@gamblersbookclub.com
www.gamblersbookclub.com

Walter Gibson was one of the most prolific writers ever, best known for his work on the pulp fiction character, *The Shadow*, but also producing classic works in a number of fields, including gambling and horseracing titles. This original work, written for the Gambler's Book Club, has been republished in various titles through the years, and remains a classic with much sought-after information that is still valid today.

T TABLE OF CONTENTS

INTRODUCTION

by Gamblers Book Club Editors

If you're serious about winning money at horseracing, this book will show you the secrets of success. You will not only learn how to pick the right horses in the right races, you'll also find out how to avoid making bad bets. Bottom line, you'll pick more winners and fewer losers, and end up at the cashier's window far more often than ever before.

Unlike games of chance such as roulette or craps where you must risk your bankroll on a lucky spin of the wheel or roll of the dice, picking the ponies is a matter of skill and judgment. This book will show you insider betting formulas for betting favorites and long shots, and the secrets of overcoming the track's fee for acting as the banker for your bets.

Relying on actual track results and the common sense approach of a pro, Gibson has analyzed what your chances of winning really are when making various types of bets—including betting on horses with middle odds, finding profitable overlays, and making shrewd picks for the daily double—and gives you winning formulas for each type of wager. In depth chapters also cover how to read daily racing forms, how to evaluate the weight factor, and how progressive betting systems work.

The goal of this book is to make you a winning player. Let Walter Gibson show you how!

1 OVERVIEW

There is an old saying that "you can't beat the races." Where the average horseplayer is concerned, that is the one thing at the racetrack that runs true to form. He is not only faced by a percentage that works steadily against him; he is apt to outguess himself as well. Always, it seems, there is a horse he should have played instead of the one he did.

That in itself is an argument in favor of system play if races are to be played at all. Unlike games of chance such as roulette, which depends on the spin of a wheel, or craps, in which hopes teeter and totter on the roll of the dice, picking the ponies can become a matter of skill and judgment. A player may at least gauge the outcome, even though he cannot actually control it.

All this hinges on the fact than in pari-mutuel betting, the legalized form at horse races today, the track acts simply as a banker for funds that a multitude of horseplayers wager against one another. For this service, it deducts approximately 15 per cent, including tax, from the amount it pays to each winner. This figure varies in different states, with about 85 percent the player's best expectancy, though more often, he keeps a little less.

To that extent, a racing pool resembles an ordinary lottery, which is another bad gamble over a long run. But again, the rule does not apply when horses are picked by judgment rather than chance. A horse that can draw away from its competition and come in first across the finish line is quite different from a slip of paper that has to be drawn from a hat.

Only a comparatively small percentage of the millions of people who patronize American tracks make exhaustive efforts to pick winners. The rest follow accepted patterns of play, or go by the opinions of professional handicappers, whose daily selections appear in newspapers or special racing publications. Some players rely on what they believe to be "inside information" sent to them via e-mail or phone, while others count on picking up "hot tips" at the track.

Also, there are many who play their own hunches, who back a horse because they like its looks or its name, or even figure out lucky numbers that they think will win. A surprisingly large number vacillate from one mode of operation to another, almost without rhyme and reason, except that they are looking for some way of betting that will pay off better than the last.

It is this potpourri of opinion that makes the odds for each race. In many races, the element of luck figures much more strongly before the horses go to the post than after they are actually off and running. Those are the races in which the public overlooks a favorite, thus giving it higher odds than it deserves; or when the favorite is overplayed, giving higher odds to other horses that are potential winners.

> **Public opinion makes the odds for each horse race.**

In theory, the perfect race is one in which a dozen horses would be well enough matched to finish almost even, but it is impossible to line up such a starting group. Even then, the condition of the horses or the track, the distance to be run, the starting positions of the horses, the jockeys who are to ride them, could all affect the calculations.

Various measures are employed to equalize each contest, such as entering horses of the same age, sex, or even estimated value. Another important factor is that of added weight, which is regarded as the best equalizer. But none of these are enough. Even before the players begin to put their money on their choices, certain horses are recognized as likely winners in a given race, while others are given only slight consideration.

Each track has its own handicapper who lists what he regards as proper approximate odds for each horse in a race. This is called the **morning line** and serves as a preliminary wagering guide. Other handicappers make their own selections, which are published in newspapers and racing journals. These graded handicaps may differ from the track man's and from each other.

The selectors also pick horses to finish in the order of first, second and third in each race. From these, newspapers and racing forms make up a consensus representing the combined choices. Many bettors are strongly influenced by the consensus, which may show various degrees of shading, where certain races are concerned.

THE TOTE BOARD

The final odds are determined by the bettors themselves. The betting windows open long enough before each race to allow all players to lay their wagers. Some, however, linger to the last moment. That is because a remarkable machine called the **totalizator** adds the early bets, tabulates them and flashes the numbers of the horses, along with their odds of the moment, on a huge bulletin board called the **tote board**.

To the avid race follower, these fluctuations are as vital as a ticker tape to a Wall Street broker. The flashing odds, registering terms as 4 to 1, 5 to 2, 2 to 1, 3 to 2, can bring a horse into low-odds classification of a **favorite**. Conversely, a well-rated nag may go skyrocketing to the realm of the **long shots**, around 10 to 1 or higher. By waiting, a player learns if these changes are merely temporary or an actual trend. Sometimes, these odds may begin to reverse themselves, or those on other horses may enter the picture.

Whatever the case, the final tote board figures stand. They represent the "human element" as personalized by the betting public. Sometimes the choice of favorites adheres to those of the selectors, as represented by the consensus. At other times it may vary, individually as well as collectively.

In the aggregate, the tote board favorites come through as winners about as often as those of the selectors. This may be attributed partly to the influence of the selectors themselves upon the betting public, and partly to the influx of big money whenever a certain horse looks like a sure bet.

There is a sound saying in racing circles: "Nobody ever lost money backing winners." So when the odds suddenly drop on a certain horse, many players jump on the bandwagon figuring they will ride right along with it. Nor do the big-time bettors worry greatly when this happens. It means they must put up more money to gain as much as they anticipated, but it makes their "sure" thing look legitimate.

There are cases to the contrary, notwithstanding, in which an odds-on favorite proves a dismal fizzle. An **odds-on horse**, it may be mentioned, is one that runs at less than even money, paying under a dollar for each dollar invested. This brings us to perhaps the most important phase of racing, and one of the least understood; namely, the matter of odds.

THE ODDS

When a newcomer to the racetrack—there are about three million of them a year—first sees the tote board, he or she is impressed by those odds of 3 to 1 and buys a $2 ticket, which, true to the rule of beginner's luck, pays off.

The tote board, however, was not exact in its statement. It only flashed 3 to 1, where the actual odds were 3.10 to 1. So the lucky winner, who expects to pick up $6, finds that his ticket brings him $8.20. Naturally, he hurries away, thinking there was a mistake; and naturally, he bets the next race, hoping there will be another mistake. But there was no mistake.

The $8.20 represents the 3.10 to 1 (or $6.20 to $2) plus the $2 which the bettor put up and therefore was entitled to receive; but it looks much bigger when he gets it back as part of the total return. This is not only deceptive; it is an incentive. It makes the player want to try again; and usually he does.

Even an odds-on payoff sounds imposing when the player collects $3.20 for a $2 mutuel ticket; but a simple subtraction shows that he is receiving only 60 cents on the dollar, multiplied by two ($1.20), plus his own $2 which is returned to him. In racing parlance, an odds-on favorite is a horse that has been "bet down" below even money, or equal odds. When a favorite is bet down so low that it pays only $2.10 on a $2 ticket, the player benefits by what is known as a **minus pool** wherein the track not only foregoes its 15 percent but may be forced to make up a difference in the player's favor, as $2.10 is a minimum pay-off.

With such a race coming up, calculating players have been known to draw sizable amounts from their savings funds, take the money out to the track and put it on the favorite, then deposit it back in the bank the next day, along with the 5 percent interest that they made on their brief investment. The only real risk, some such players avow, is in carrying all that money to and from the track.

One bad guess, however, and it might take a player a few years to make up the deficit, if he could at all. From this type of play, in which a large amount is risked for an almost sure, but small return, we run the gamut to the other extreme, wherein a small amount is wagered in hope of a 100 to 1 return—or more—which is very seldom realized.

In between are many degrees that depend on various ways of betting as well as styles or systems of play. Of prime consideration are the possible types of wagers, which come under the headings of straight, place and show. The next chapter covers each type of bet players can make at race tracks.

2 HOW RACES ARE BET

In many races, excitement rises after the horses leave the starting gate and reaches a fever pitch as they round the final turn of the oval track and come down the straight home stretch to the finish line. Two horses are running neck to neck, with the rest bunched well behind. One horse noses out the other at the wire and a triumphant shout comes from its frenzied backers, drowning out the moan that accompanies the tearing of hair and tickets by the disappointed followers of the other steed.

But this tells only part of the story. Among the crowd are groups of happy bettors who do not care which of the two horses win, as they will cash in their tickets anyway. There are still more who aren't watching the finish at all. They are interested in the remaining horses, hoping that one will draw away from the rest of the pack and finish third. To their way of thinking and betting, that is just as good as having the horse come in first or second; in some cases, even better.

The reason is that a horse doesn't always have to win a race for its backers to win money. That is because there are three ways to play a horse:

- **Straight**, which means betting that the horse will come in first;
- **Place**, betting that the horse will finish first or second;
- **Show**, which pays off if the horse finishes first, second or third.

Sometimes the term **win** is used instead of **straight**, serving as a reminder that a horse must win in order to pay off on a straight bet. Backing a horse to win is called betting it **on the nose**. Horses that come in first, second or third, are said to be **in the money**, which is true, provided a player has bet them accordingly.

It would be very neat if these modes of betting could be figured proportionately on a strict one-two-three basis. But **place** and **show** bets are not calculated from the odds posted on straight wagers. Each has its own individual pool, which is registered on the tote board, giving the number of wagers made on each horse, the figures fluctuating like those of the win pool.

No approximate odds are posted on place or show because they are determined by what happens with two or three horses, not just one. At the finish of the race, the total place pool is divided into two equal portions and the money in each half is distributed among the players whose horses finished first and second.

Similarly, the show pool is cut into thirds and disbursed among the backers of all three "money" horses. This results in varied proportions where such bets are concerned, dependent on the mood of the betting public, which differs at many tracks, some favoring a more conservative play than others.

Some players use the rule that whatever the odds paid on a straight bet, place should pay about half, and show should pay one-third. This is a fairly good index for calculating bets around the 3 to 1 level, particularly where a place bet is concerned, though a show bet is apt to lag. For example, a horse rated at 3 to 1 straight, would be 3 to 2 to place and 1 to 1 (even money) to show. On a pari-mutuel $2 ticket, payoffs would be $8 straight, $5 place, $4 show. Actual races, however, give such returns as:

ACTUAL RETURNS ON 3 TO 1 HORSE		
STRAIGHT	PLACE	SHOW
$8.00	$4.80	$3.40
8.00	5.00	3.40
8.00	5.00	3.00
8.00	5.20	3.80
8.00	4.80	3.40

Going higher, a horse rated at 6 to 1 straight, would be 3 to 1 to place, and 2 to 1 to show. Here, the place bets also begin to sag. On a pari-mutuel $2 ticket, payoffs would be $14 straight, $8 place, $6 show. Some typical returns are as follows:

ACTUAL RETURNS ON 6 TO 1 HORSE		
STRAIGHT	PLACE	SHOW
$14.00	$5.80	$4.20
14.00	6.80	5.10
14.00	5.20	3.80

In all instances, these returns include the original $2 bet. The variations, of course, are due to the different sizes of the place and show pools.

BETTING TO WIN

Betting to win is recommended by many veteran players as the only type of wager to use. They point out that a straight bet gives higher odds than any other type and therefore promises greater profit. They reduce all betting to two simple factors: aiming for solid winners and looking for horses that offer a good price. Such players say that nobody ever went broke backing winners, and they try to make their money bring the greatest possible return. If a race is doubtful, they either pass it up or go all out for a horse that looks reasonably good and is running at unusually high odds.

Various systems are based on this type of betting, all seeking to eliminate some of the losing races that are bound to occur, or to increase the percentage of wins on any risky races that are played at higher odds.

BETTING TO PLACE

Betting to place is popular among certain players under suitable conditions. In a race where one horse is recognized as an almost certain winner, the real contest is for second place. Therefore, picking a horse to place is like backing a winner in an average race, and may prove quite as profitable.

There are races, too, in which the choice is a tossup between two outstanding horses. Because of the uncertainty, neither horse is apt to be overbet and both may be running at fairly good odds. By betting his choice to place, a player stands to make a reasonable return whether his horse comes in first or second.

Some players may back both horses to place in such a situation, on the chance that they will finish one-two, yielding a double payoff. The danger here is that too many other players may be swayed by the same uncertainty and that the place betting will be too heavy. For example, at a Western track, two horses were bet down far below the others, one at straight odds of 1.20 to 1, the other at 2.90 to 1. The horses came in one-two but the place odds were only .40 to 1 and .50 to 1.

A winning $2 ticket on horse A paid a straight $4.40, while a place ticket on horse A paid $2.80 and a place ticket on horse B paid $3.00. Here an investment of $4 brought only a $5.80 return, which was not worth the added risk.

Betting an odds-on favorite to place is a much safer and sometimes more profitable procedure. In another race at the same track, one horse was bet down to .80 to 1 and came through a winner, paying $3.60 on a $2 straight ticket. But the betting was so much lighter for the horse to place, that its odds in that department only came to .90 to 1. So the horse paid $3.80 on a $2 place ticket, which would have been just as good if it had finished second!

Another advantage of place betting is that losing streaks are shorter than with straight bets. The pay-offs are only about half as large, but the losing streaks are only half as long. This is important in betting systems where the player keeps increasing his wagers on a progressive basis after every loss until he strikes a win.

BETTING TO SHOW

Betting to show is the most conservative bet of all. It is recommended for players who want the fun of betting with small risk. The payoffs are too slight to show much profit on low-priced horses; and with horses at very high odds, which are known as long shots, too many players are apt to bet them to show, thus cutting the odds too much. For example, at an Eastern track, a horse won a race at odds of 35.50 to 1. Place paid only 9.30 to 1, which was bad enough, but the show price was even worse, a mere 4.30 to 1. Payoff on a $2 mutuel was $73.00 straight, $20.60 place, and $10.60 show, which wasn't enough for a horse that should not have finished in the money.

With odds-on horses, betting to show is a real insurance bet, sometimes giving the player the advantage of a minus pool. Here is an example of a good show bet: A favorite in a six-horse race was running at .70 to 1, with half of the other horses in the long-shot category of 12 to 1 or higher. The horse was bet down to .15 to 1 to show, but one of the long shots came through and the favorite finished third.

The result was a $2.30 payoff on a $2 show ticket, despite the favorite's poor performance. In another race at the same track on the same day, a .60 to 1 favorite failed to win in a five-horse race. This time, the show bet paid $2.10 on a $2 ticket that represented a minus pool.

Such winnings are small, but almost certain, and show bets frequently pay off at place prices with an odds-on favorite. Even when paying less than one-third the amount of straight wagers, betting to show cuts down losing streaks to one-third, which is a great help in some forms of progressive betting.

COMBINATION BETS

Combination bets involve a three-way ticket including straight, place and show. This type of betting is most easily figured on a $6 basis, with a $2 bet each way. The player collects on all three if the nag wins; on place and show if it comes in second; on show only, if it finishes third.

While many players seem to like this style of play, it is seldom used in systematic wagering, at least not in the rigid form just described. The purpose of a combination bet is to cushion the losses on straight wagers by collecting enough on place to get back the investment. In that case, a player may prefer to bet $2 straight and $4 to place in each race. If he decides to use show bets to carry the ball when both straight and place miss out, his bets might run $2, $4, $6; or $2, $4, $8; or in some other proportions. He could buy a combination ticket if he wanted, but he would have to buy additional tickets for place and show.

The argument against any form of combination betting is that the player would do better to put his money in the most productive column: straight, place or show. If he winds up a series of races $80 ahead on straight play, but $10 out on place and $22 out on show, he obviously would have made a much bigger profit—$240 to be exact—if he had made all straight bets instead of trying it three ways.

But the fallacy is that the player has no way of knowing beforehand which column is going to prove the most productive. If he knew, he wouldn't need to use them all. He might even have guessed wrong and made all his wagers to show, with a resultant loss of $66.

There are certain types of play that lend themselves to straight, place or show betting, as the case may be, along lines already mentioned. But most of these are so obviously geared to one pattern that it would be foolish to bet them in any other way. So a player shouldn't be buying a combination ticket in the first place, unless reasonably sure that straight, place or show have about equal chances of coming up with the highest profit.

In racing parlance, a player who buys a combination ticket is betting **across the board**.

THE DAILY DOUBLE

This is a special type of wager popular at many tracks, but generally frowned upon by system players, though the **daily double** has its own modes of play. The player buys a ticket bearing the number of a horse in the first race and another with the number of a horse in the second race. If both prove to be winners, he cashes in his ticket, sometimes on a grand scale.

The daily double has its own pool, which is divided among the players who call the two shots correctly. Picking a winner in one race but not in the other is no good. A bet is lost if either fails to come through. At some tracks, daily doubles are run on different pairs of races.

QUINELLA

A **quinella** is simply a form of betting two horses to place in the same race, but in this case both must come through, finishing in one-two order. Otherwise, as with the daily double, the bet is lost.

One specific race is listed for quinella play. It has its own special pool made up of the two-horse bets that are wagered for that purpose only.

PICK SIX

The **pick six** is an extension of the daily double that is gaining popularity among some horseplayers. Working on the usual $2 minimum, a bettor picks a winner for each of six specified races. If all his choices come through, he cashes in heavily, as the pick six has its own pari-mutuel pool like the daily double.

OPTIONAL BETS

Optional betting methods are available to players who choose to use them. These include the following:

Parlays, wherein a player lets winnings from one race ride on the next. He may carry it on through further races, varying the type of bets (straight, place or show).

"If" bets, wherein when a player loses a race, he stakes a specified sum on another horse in an effort to recoup.

Progression betting, which calls for regular increases of wagers on certain races, as opposed to flat bets, in which the same amount is played on each race.

Now that we have reviewed the many types of bets a player may make at the track, let us discuss the ultimate object of going to the races—picking winners. The next chapter on choosing which races to bet is just the beginning of how to ultimately pick a winner.

3 PICKING THE RACES

One of the first steps in picking a winning horse is to pick the type of race in which potential winners are most easily identified. In fact, some betting systems depend upon the choice of certain races or the elimination of others.

Generally speaking, races fall into the following categories.

SWEEPSTAKES OR STAKES RACES

Sweepstakes or **stakes races** are so called because stakes are posted by the owners and are swept by the horses that come in one-two-three-four. Players who back the right horses to win, place or show come in for a profit, too, but only the owner gets paid for a steed that finishes fourth. In the bigger and more important stakes, the track puts up an additional sum, which increases the winning urge on the part of the owners, who share proportionately according to the finish and still stand to lose their original investment when a horse only comes in fifth.

Experts maintain that class decides the best stakes races. It isn't just a case of a horse being up to form. He has to have it or he shouldn't be entered. According to one estimate, 80 percent of the high-grade stakes races are won by the horse that was rated to finish either first or second.

When a race has a top-heavy favorite, betting it to place or show is regarded as an investment by some players with big bankrolls. When an outsider wins, it is generally a horse that was really overlooked.

A **derby** is a stakes race run by three-year-old horses. A **cup race** is for three-year-olds and up. A **maturity** is confined to four-year olds. A **futurity** is a stakes race run by horses that were still unborn when they were entered.

HANDICAP RACES

Some sweepstakes are called **handicap races**. In these, a track handicapper assigns weights to the different horses in order to equalize their speed and produce a close finish. These weights are based on past performances and other factors that work to that result, the heavier weights going to the better horses.

At larger tracks, which attract outstanding horses, experienced handicappers can do a thorough and effective job. Picking winners demands much study on the part of players at such tracks. At lesser ovals, the caliber of the horses is much more doubtful, allowing corresponding leeway on the part of speculative bettors. This applies still more strongly to allowance races.

ALLOWANCE RACES

In all types of races, concessions in weight are given in accordance with generally prescribed conditions. In **allowance races**, they are determined by the amount of money won over a certain period, or the lack of money won. That is, the horse that has given the poorest performance or registered the least number of wins is granted the greatest reduction in weight.

The idea is to bring competitive horses together by mingling the good with the bad, under conditions suitable to both. The conditions of such races vary according to the different tracks and also to the availability of suitable horses, as there are no set rules. For some horses, an allowance race is a step up to a higher bracket; for others, it is a chance to stage a comeback.

CLAIMING RACES

Claiming races represent the majority of all races, with price the determining figure. Every horse entered in the race is automatically put up for sale and may be claimed at the established price by any bona fide buyer. The claim is deposited in a sealed box before the race is run, and it stands, win or lose, even if the horse drops dead before it reaches the finish line!

The claiming price is in itself an equalizer. An owner will not run a $5,000 horse in a $2,500 claiming race, because buyers would snap it up immediately and the owner would lose the difference. Conversely, a $2,500 horse would not be entered in a $5,000 claiming race. as it would be completely outclassed.

Horses are constantly being stepped up or down, which has a definite effect on the betting. Normally, an owner does not drop a horse to a lower bracket unless he is eager for a win or is willing to let it go, even as a bargain.

Conversely, a horse may be pushed up the scale because it is showing enough improvement to make it worth more. Some claiming races include horses of different values, the cheaper group being given a special weight allowance. In optional claiming races, an owner may enter a horse against those of approximate value, without offering it for sale.

A claiming race may also be an allowance race, or even a handicap race, attracting horses of a better caliber than the cheap **platers**, as horses that habitually run in claiming races

are termed. Weight figures strongly in such races, but the claiming price is an ever-present factor.

Generally speaking, claiming races are among the least predictable, as they are run by poorer horses, and changes of ownership and training conditions may have a bearing on their performances along with ups or downs in claiming prices.

Statistics from major tracks indicate that the average of winning favorites is lower in claiming races than in other types, but the odds are usually higher.

MAIDEN RACES

Maiden races are run by horses that have never won a race. The term "maiden" applies to either sex. Many horses go through their entire careers without a win; hence some bettors regard maiden races as the least predictable of all. Horses of specific age groups are brought together in maiden races. These events may be claiming or allowance races, though there is little to go by in the granting of allowances, due to the lack of wins.

Statistics from major tracks give a high percentage of winning favorites in maiden races, due perhaps to the quality of the horses running on such ovals. Maiden races at secondary tracks are apt to be cluttered by chronic losers, making it all the more difficult to pick a winner.

One thing is sure about these races—there will be one less maiden at the finish, as they can't lose!

STEEPLECHASE AND HURDLE RACES

Steeplechase or **hurdle races** are run over special courses at some of the larger tracks. The participating horses are termed **jumpers** because they must clear hedges and ditches in a steeplechase, while hurdles are set up as hazards in a hurdle race. Many system players ignore such races entirely, sticking to flat racing, as the common non-jumping races are styled.

With this discussion of the types of races typically run at tracks across the country, let us delve into how to read the racing charts, those masterpieces of condensed facts so aptly abbreviated to preserve space and patience.

4 HOW TO READ RACING CHARTS

Many daily newspapers run charts giving the results of the previous day's races, and these are quite as easy to read as the box scores of baseball games, or the details of other athletic events. Readers soon become familiar with the racing terms and their abbreviations; hence constant reference to such charts is a valuable guide to future play.

THE BASIC TERMS AND MEANINGS

Often the results are given in condensed form, stating the type of races, which horses finished in the money, the names of the losing horses and a few other pertinent facts. These are too meager for real analysis, but serve as a basis to which other data should be added. For example, beneath the name of the racetrack the following might appear:

FIRST-$2,800, cl., 3YO and up, 6f.			
Happy Melody (Rogers)	$5.80	3.60	2.90
Baluchistan (Barry)	....	13.20	7.20
Dom Pedro (Landis)	....	....	3.00
Time-1:12 3-5. Cannonball, Presto, Nice Baby, Uncle Walt, Egyptian Prince, Durango, China Doll also ran.			

Translated, this means that the first race was for a $2,800 purse, that it was a claiming (cl.) race, that the horses were three-year-olds (3YO) and up, and that the distance was six furlongs (6f.) or three-quarters of a mile.

The winning horse was Happy Melody, ridden by a jockey named Rogers. It paid $5.80 for a $2 bet if played to win, $3.60 if played to place, and $2.90 if played to show. Baluchistan came in second, ridden by a jockey named Barry. It failed to pay if played to win; however, the horse paid $13.20 for a place ticket, and $7.20 for a show ticket. Dom Pedro came in third, ridden by Landis. This horse failed to pay if played to win or place, but cashed in to the tune of $3 for a show ticket.

The winning horse ran the six furlongs in one minute, twelve and three-fifth seconds, as indicated by "Time-1:12 3-5." Following the three horses that were in the money, the remaining horses finished in the order given, and paid nothing, as indicated by the term **also ran**.

The results list the races in order through the entire card, and running down the list are abbreviations that are almost self-explanatory. Some forego the amounts of the purse. Others insert the notation: "Off-2:55½," meaning that the race started at thirty seconds after 2:55 p.m.

MORE TERMS AND MEANINGS

Here are some further samples of notations and their meanings. The term "allow" refers to an "allowance race." The term "2YO" obviously stands for "two-year-old," while "mdns" refers to "maidens." Instead of "6f." a chart may read "6 fur" for six furlongs. Other understandable abbreviations are "1m" for one mile; "1 M 70 yds" for one mile and seventy yards; and so on.

After the second race, you may find the statement: Double (3-7) paid $58.60. This means that the winning horse in the first race was number 3 on the program, while the winner of the second race was number 7. Lucky holders of daily double tickets with those numbers collected $58.60 for each $2 invested.

Races run on turf are so designated, and at the head of the list or at the bottom, there is usually a statement such as "weather clear; track fast," which is vital information to the bettor who is appraising the comparative abilities of certain horses.

An added item at the bottom of the results column may state: Attendance: 16,834 Handle: $1,122,684

The term "attendance" is self-explanatory, while **handle**, which is short for **pari-mutuel handle**, refers to the amount of money wagered. This is rather good to know, because small attendance, with a proportionately low handle, may affect the odds of certain horses. Perhaps that is why those figures are set at the very top of more elaborate charts, which in turn supply more vital information all down the line. These appear in many newspapers and are avidly devoured by racing fans, who may find clues to future prospects through the statistics provided.

In claiming races, these specify the claiming prices, an important factor if a certain horse is going up or down in value. In each race, all horses are listed under the heading of "starters," followed by the weight (abbreviated "wt.") that each horse carried.

The post position (abbreviated P.P.) is given for each horse, and following that, a series of cross columns tell how they ran from start to finish. The expanded chart following covers the first race already listed. This lists the starting horses, the weights they carried, and their post positions. The term "st." gives each horse's position immediately after the start, which is valuable to know, as it may tell which horses are fast starters, and may explain a poor showing by a highly rated horse that got off to a slow start, such as Nice Baby in this particular race. Post positions are figured from the rail at the inside of the track outward, and this should be taken into consequence when picturing all that happened at the start.

The column headed "¼" gives the running positions when the horses have reached the quarter-mile mark. Here it is possible to estimate the distances between them in terms of "lengths." Thus Dom Pedro, listed at 11 was in first position at the quarter-mile, approximately his own length ahead of Cannonball, listed at 2½ signifying that he was half his length ahead of Happy Melody, running third. Note that Presto is listed as 5hd, meaning that he had a margin of a horse's head over the next horse, Nice Baby.

Under "⅜" we find the running positions at the half-mile mark, which are similarly interpreted. The column "str." refers to the "stretch" or straightaway leading to the finish line. The "stretch call" is generally made at the "eighth pole," which is an eighth of a mile short of the finish. In a six-furlong race, the horses would therefore have run about five-eighths of a mile.

The term "fin." represents the finish, and here, in addition to "hd" for "head," abbreviations of "nk" for "neck" and "no" for "nose" are fairly frequent, as positions may be decided by such narrow margins. The listing of "times" below the chart refers to the running times of the leading horse at the quarter-mile, half-mile, and finish respectively. A fifth of a second is added for each length to learn the speeds of the other horses. Thus Happy Melody finished in 1:12 3-5, two lengths ahead of Baluchistan, who therefore ran the distance in 1:13.

Every horse's time can thereby be approximately gauged, except for those following the statement **scratched**, which means that they did not run, though originally scheduled to do so.

This chart also gives the names of all jockeys with the horses they rode. The returns for straight (st.), place (pl.), and show (sh.) are the same as in the modified chart, but the fuller version has other important data in the column headed "Odds $1."

That lists the exact odds on each and every horse. The odds on Happy Melody to win were 1.90 to 1, which would have flashed 2 to 1 on the tote board. A $2 bet brought a gain of $3.80, which, added to the wager, enabled the player to collect $5.80.

Note that Baluchistan ran at 11.60 to 1 and Dom Pedro at 2.10 to 1. Those odds applied if either came in first. So Baluchistan was rated at 12 to 1, and Dom Pedro at 2 to 1. All the remaining horses were also rated as to winning odds, which are figures that are valuable in comparing horses in future races.

EXPANDED RACING CHART

STARTERS	WT.	P.P.	ST.	¼	½	STR.	FIN.	JOCKEYS	ST.	PL.	SH.	ODDS $1
Happy Melody	117	3	6	3¹	4²	2ʰᵈ	1²	Rogers	5.80	3.60	2.90	1.90
Baluchistan	115	7	10	9²	8²	4²	2½	Barry	...	13.20	7.20	11.60
Dom Pedro	119	2	3	1¹	2¹	3²	3ⁿᵒ	Landis	...	...	3.00	2.10
Cannonball	117	6	1	2½	1¹	1¹	4 2½	A. Boni	...	...	...	7.80
Presto	119	9	4	5ʰᵈ	5½	5²	5ⁿᵏ	Marvin	...	...	...	17.90
Nice Baby	115	8	9	6½	6³	7²	6²	Cooke	...	...	...	3.20
Uncle Walt	117	10	2	4³	3¹	6ʰᵈ	7ʰᵈ	Ritz	...	...	...	6.60
Egypt. Prince	112	1	7	10	7½	8³	8²	C. Boni	...	...	...	21.50
Durango	110	5	8	8²	9³	9³	9⁶	Beaum't	...	...	...	42.90
China Doll	117	4	5	7ʰᵈ	10	10	10	Dunn	...	...	...	70.60

Times–0:23 1-5; 0:47 3-5; 1:12 3-5.

Scratched–Hurricane, Weeping Willow.

Still more data appear in these charts, particularly in those printed in racing publications such as *The Daily Racing Form*. Full conditions of each race are spelled out, names of owners are listed, and the winner's pedigree is given, with a description of the steed itself. Here again, abbreviations are used, such as "dk. b. or br. c. 3" for "dark bay or brown colt, three years old" or "ch. g. 5" for "chestnut gelding, five years old," and so on.

The abbreviation "b" under the heading "equipment" indicates that the horse wore blinkers; "s" denotes that the jockey wore spurs; and sometimes "w" is included in this special column, denoting that a whip was carried, though this is so common that it is often deleted as superfluous.

A description of the race is given beneath the chart, mentioning whether horses faltered, weakened, or showed proper response. Interference and mishaps are noted, furnishing the racing fan with other items for future consideration.

Occasionally, abbreviations such as "D" occur in charts to indicate that a horse was disqualified and placed in the position listed, or "DH" to signify that two horses finished nose to nose in a "dead heat" and thereby tied for that position.

Two or more horses owned by the same stable, or having the same trainer, are listed with the letter "a" in the "Odds $1 column, as "a-3.20" on each horse. This classifies them as an "entry" and they are considered as one horse where the betting is concerned. Another such entry in the same race is coupled with the letter "b" in the same column.

When there are more than twelve horses in a race, the "outside" horses, or sometimes others, may be treated as an entry called the "field" and treated as a single betting unit. The listing "f" on the "Odds $1" column is used with such horses.

PAST PERFORMANCE CHARTS

Once you are familiar with result charts, you are ready to graduate to the **past performance charts**, which appear in daily racing publications. These are condensations of result charts covering the horse's performances over as many as a dozen races, each being listed in a single line, with as many as thirty columns. The data of each race is listed, also its number on the card and the racetrack, which is duly abbreviated as "Aqu" for Aqueduct, "CD" for Churchill Downs, "SA" for Santa Anita, "TrP" for Tropical Park, and so on.

The condition of the track is listed as "fst" for fast, "gd" for good, "hy" for heavy, "my" for muddy, "sl" for slow, "sly" for sloppy. Types of races have such abbreviations as "alw" for allowance, "cl" for claiming, "hcp" for handicap, "md" for maiden, "spl wt" for special weight, and others. The distance of each race is also specified.

Times of leading horses are given, followed by the positions of the individual horse in relation to the leader. The jockey, the equipment, the weight carried, and the odds on the horse all appear in following columns. The three horses that finished in the money are listed, and the number of starters is specified.

There will be ten such charts for a ten-horse race, each a graphic record of an individual horse, giving the avid fan a chance for detailed comparison without having to check the charts of all the races in which the contestants previously appeared. Familiarity with such charts is needed to read them and to recognize special symbols. However, they are explained in the racing publications, or in special brochures that they supply to readers.

Racing journals also list recent **workouts** of individual horses, giving the name of the track and the distance over which a horse in training was run against time, which in turn is specified, as, for example, three furlongs in 38 1-5. Here, the manner of the workout is abbreviated: "b" for breezing, "d" for driving, "e" for easily, "h" for handily, "u" for eased up. These workouts may indicate whether a horse has retained or improved its form, and are therefore of value in conjunction with the past performance charts.

Now we will more forward one more step in learning how to pick winners. The next chapter covers four ways you can either win or lose in making your picks. Hopefully, by the end of the chapter, you will have learned to pick winners, passing the losers in the backstretch.

5 PICKING HORSES

All betting methods have one long-range aim—to beat down the 15 percent advantage that the track holds over the player. You must remember this in picking horses. Simply put, unless your choice has what appears to be a better than average chance to win, it is generally wise to pass up that race.

"You can beat a race, but you can't beat the races" is an old saying that's been going around for decades. This is self-contradictory to a degree because if a player can beat one race, he can beat another, or another until he lines up enough of them, in which case he will be beating the races, no mistake about it. But hoping to beat every race, or all the races, is obviously too much.

> Hoping to beat every race is too much to expect.

Players who want a lot of action will ordinarily go out to win a lot of races that they should avoid. So if a system or method of play merely cuts down some of that troublesome 15-percent burden, the fault may be the player's own. The point to remember is that missing out on a few winners won't hurt, if it means missing out on a still greater proportion of losers.

Picking suitable horses is preliminary to betting on them, so the first step is to consider ways in which a player goes about winning.

1. PLAYING THE FAVORITES

Here, the player goes along with the adage, "Nobody ever went broke betting on winners." The idea is to win so often that you can't lose in the long run, because the percentage of profit outweighs that of losses. This means backing the favorites, horses which have the lowest odds on the tote board, or which are picked to win their races by a majority of competent selectors. Often, this is the same horse in each case.

The low odds do not matter if the choices come through as winners; in fact, the lower the odds, the higher the percentage of wins, as a rule. But the margin is usually unfavorable to the player.

Statistics show that slightly less than one-third of the favorites come through as winners; that about one-half finish second; and perhaps two-thirds may be counted on to finish third. So they would have to average $6 to win, $4 to place, and $3 to show, for the player to break even. Unfortunately the favorites are apt to run at less than 2 to 1 on most tracks, with proportionately low odds for place and show; or when the odds go higher, the favorites fail to finish in the money as often as they normally should.

As a simple example, a random run of eighty races at an Eastern track produced 23 wins (29%), altogether paying off $127.50; exactly 40 places (50%), paying off $141.80; and 51 shows (64%), paying off $138.10. Inasmuch as the player had to put up $160 in each type of bet, it is obvious he could not make money that way.

At a Southern track, a random run of forty-eight races brought 15 wins (31%), which paid off $75.20; exactly 24 places (50%), which paid off $83.20; and 28 shows (58%), which brought $80.10. In each case, an investment of $96 was necessary to bring back the lesser total. Here, the place and show wagers made dents in the track's 15 percent profit, but not enough to break even.

The system player endeavors to turn such loss into profit by eliminating the more doubtful races, or by switching from a favorite to a close contender that may have equal chances, but be giving better odds. When selectors disagree among themselves or with the tote board, there is always the chance that a false favorite is monopolizing the bets. Finding the real favorite can then prove profitable.

2. LOOKING FOR LONG SHOTS

Nobody has to look far for long shots. They are the horses whose odds climb up to astronomical figures. If a player happens to hit one that pays, say 100 to 1, he can bet a lot of races with the track's money until he runs out of cash or hits another such winner. The weakness of playing long shots is that many horses running at 20 to 1 and upward should not be in the race at all. To fill a card, such horses often must be included, but they might just as well be rated at 1,000 to 1, they have so little chance to win.

One meeting at an American track was replete with long shots, with some races including two or three horses above the 100 to 1 mark—and one nag running at nearly 500 to 1. Yet, out of more than a hundred races that were run, in only one did the horse with the highest odds come home a winner, and that was at a mere 18 to 1 that paid $38 on a $2 straight ticket.

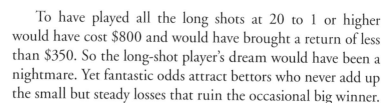
To have played all the long shots at 20 to 1 or higher would have cost $800 and would have brought a return of less than $350. So the long-shot player's dream would have been a nightmare. Yet fantastic odds attract bettors who never add up the small but steady losses that ruin the occasional big winner.

Systematic long-shot play may begin with minimum odds at some set figure, as 7 to 1, 10 to 1, or even 15 to 1. The player then considers all horses at higher odds than his established mark and backs those that qualify according to the system's rules. Mere price is never the sole factor, nor does the horse with the highest odds have to be considered.

3. BETTING OVERLAYS

These are usually "in-between" horses that offer tidy and satisfactory profits. A horse becomes an **underlay** when its tote board odds drop below a well-estimated figure. It becomes an **overlay** when it rises above such a level. Some players use the morning line as a standard; others watch for a sudden climb of the tote board odds themselves.

This is often the result of a drop in odds on some other horse, which may turn a mere contender into a tote board favorite, so that the original favorite becomes an overlay. At times, the public may be justified in giving one horse the go-by, but on the contrary, bettors may follow the advice of an over-optimistic selector or may simply join a stampede that produces low odds on the wrong horse.

That's when the smart bettors look for the right nag among the overlays and risk their bankrolls accordingly. It is not a case of aiming for a sure win, but an effort to cash in more heavily than anticipated if a likely win comes through. An average number of wins will yield a steady profit to a long-range player who is good at spotting overlays.

Various systems have been built around this type of betting. In simplest form, suppose that three horses should be rated at 6 to 1. Due to vagaries of players, they show on the tote board as 4 to 1, 5 to 1 and 8 to 1. The 8 to 1 horse is bet as the overlay; if it wins, the player will receive $18 for his $2 ticket, or $4 more than he would get from a $14 pay-off on a 6 to 1 horse. This is also $8 more than the potential $10 pay-off that the 4 to 1 horse might bring.

Technically, many favorites are underlays, but still are worth betting as solid choices. Conversely, some long shots are actually overlays, but are too uncertain to be risked. Price plus prospects are the elements of the true overlay.

4. PROGRESSION BETTING

This generally means increasing the amount of each wager after a specified number of losses, and reducing the amount after each win. This enables the winners to pay up for some of the losers, if the play runs true to form. So a certain regularity or frequency of wins is necessary, whether the player is betting straight, place or show.

Progression betting is a form of system play in itself, if bets are made hit or miss; but such wagering is apt to prove disastrous. Therefore, progressions are usually geared to some steady or conservative system, such as the play of recognized favorites. The general rule is that any method of play that results in only a slight win or loss on equal wagers—or on a "flat bet" basis—will bring substantial profits when a progression is applied.

Progressions, therefore, form a special subject in themselves and will be treated as such under their own headings in the next chapter.

6 SEVEN SYSTEMS FOR PICKING WINNERS

1. THE SELECTIVE TOTE BOARD SYSTEM

This is a simple method of combining expert advice with public opinion, the purpose being to increase the winning percentage on the low-priced favorites. When effective, it eliminates some of the "almosts" from the almost certain winners, bringing a proportionate overall profit.

In each race, check the consensus of winning selections in a newspaper or racing sheet. Either that, or go by the choice of a well-recognized handicapper. That is the horse to play, if the race is played at all. In order to qualify, the horse must have strong public backing as well. This is determined by watching the tote board until just before post time. Two factors are required: First, the odds on the chosen horse must drop as low as 2 to 1; next, no other horse can have odds under 4 to 1. This shows that the betting public is accepting the selection in two ways, supporting the choice and ignoring any opposition.

Since frequency of profit is the aim in this system, most players will prefer to play it across the board due to the low return, although it can be played straight place or show.

In the sample results that follow, it is assumed that all three are being played on a one-two-three basis; namely, $2 straight,

$4 to place, and $6 to show. All numbers are expressed as dollars.

SELECTIVE TOTE BOARD SYSTEM VS CONSENSUS BETTING						
	SYSTEM			ALL CONSENSUS FAVORITES (NINE RACES EACH DAY)		
	STR.	PLACE	SHOW	STR.	PLACE	SHOW
FIRST DAY						
3rd Race	4.40	6.40	9.00			
4th Race	4.00	6.80	8.40			
7th Race	3.50	5.40	7.80			
			Day Totals:	11.90	46.20	63.00
SECOND DAY						
2nd Race	5.40	6.40	8.10			
5th Race	...	5.80	7.20			
			Day Totals:	10.50	25.40	43.80
THIRD DAY						
No Play						
			Day Totals:	7.00	38.60	45.00
FOURTH DAY						
No Play						
			Day Totals:	20.30	35.40	66.00
FIFTH DAY						
1st Race	6.30	7.20	9.00			
4th Race	5.10	7.20	8.40			
5th Race	...	5.00	6.90			
6th Race	5.10	6.40	7.50			
			Day Totals:	23.10	39.60	65.70
TOTAL	33.80	56.60	72.30	72.80	185.20	283.50
Less Bets	18.00	36.00	54.00	90.00	180.00	270.00
LOSS				17.20		
PROFIT	15.80	20.60	18.30		5.20	13.50
TOTAL PROFIT	$54.70			$1.50		

This represents a difference of $53.40 to the player's advantage, by using the tote board method of confirming the consensus selections. That, however, is only part of the story. Actually, there were only nine races played by the system, as opposed to the full forty-five that could have been bet on the consensus favorites. A player putting up five times the amount necessary to back all the races, and applying it only to the system bets, would have shown a profit of $273.50.

That would have required a wager of $60 ($10 straight, $20 to place, $30 to show) on each race played. In this instance, it would have worked to perfection, as a win was recorded on the first try (3rd Race, First Day) and put the player ahead of the game to stay. In only two of the nine races did the selected horse fail to win, and in each of those, the player got his money back through returns from place and show.

In playing this system, allowance may be made for late fluctuations in the tote board. Note the #1 Race, Fifth Day, for an example. Final odds on the horse were 2.10 to 1, which would have shown as 2 to 1 on the totalizer, but this bet could have been placed if the odds had shown as low as 5 to 2, provided that all other horses were clearly above the 4 to 1 mark.

In contrast, if a player is ready to head for the ticket window and put his money on a horse that appears to be an odds-on favorite, well below the 2 to 1 mark, he should not be deterred if another horse slips just under 4 to 1, and flashes at 7 to 2. But if the gap shows signs of closing further, the race should be skipped.

If the favorite is scratched, the race should automatically be passed up, unless the second choice of the consensus was rated very close to the first, in which case it can be accepted as the favorite. In listings of all consensus favorites, we have assumed that second choices would be played if firsts were scratched, and that third choices would be played if the first two were scratched.

Now let's study another five-day series of races at a different track where the results proved much less favorable. (See table following.) Here, the outcome is little more than breaking even, in fact not that good, if running expenses for the player, not the horses are included in the deal. But the system at least shows a plus, whereas an all-out play on the selected favorites would sink the bettor by more than $100 on the $2-$4-$6 scale.

The actual difference between tote board eliminations and all-out play is $118.30 in the example just given, but the mere $10.40 profit raises the question: How far in the hole is the player likely to go?

In this instance, not too far.

At the end of the fourth wager, the system player was only $16 out, beyond the original $12, meaning that he would need an initial capital of $28 or more in order to wager on the fifth race.

From there on, the system holds its own, finally coming up with a small profit. Insurance is needed, however, against still more early losses, so that the sinking fund should be five times or more the amount of the original bet, or at least $60 if flat bets are to be made at $2-$4-$6. This stresses the importance of the place and show bets, which in the above example carried the burden over a series of ten plays that produced only one payoff on a straight play. This is rather unusual where such low-odds horses are concerned, but the player should be ready for it.

Normally, this system should prove more reliable at larger tracks where the betting is heavier, because they attract horses of high caliber whose races show good consistency, an important point when hoping for a "sure win."

	SYSTEM PLAY			ALL CONSENSUS FAVORITES (NINE RACES EACH DAY)		
	STR.	PLACE	SHOW	STR.	PLACE	SHOW
FIRST DAY						
3rd Race	3.00	5.80	7.50			
			Day Totals:	11.40	22.20	29.10
SECOND DAY						
4th Race	...	7.00	8.70			
6th Race	...	...	...			
7th Race	...	...	...			
8th Race	4.80	6.60	7.80			
9th Race	...	8.60	9.60			
			Day Totals:	15.40	27.00	40.50
THIRD DAY						
2nd Race	...	...	8.40			
4th Race	...	6.80	9.30			
7th Race	...	...	8.70			
9th Race	...	6.20	8.10			
			Day Totals:	5.50	19.00	59.40
FOURTH DAY						
2nd Race	...	...	...			
8th Race	3.80	5.40	7.50			
9th Race	3.80	5.60	7.80			
			Day Totals:	13.60	27.60	43.50
FIFTH DAY						
5th Race	...	6.40	8.10			
6th Race	3.90	6.60	8.10			
8th Race	4.60	6.80	8.10			
			Day Totals:	8.50	38.00	71.40
TOTAL	23.90	71.80	107.70	54.40	133.80	243.95
Less Bets	32.00	64.00	96.00	90.00	180.00	270.00
LOSS	8.10			35.60	46.20	26.15
PROFIT		7.80	11.70			
TOTAL PROFIT	$11.40					
TOTAL LOSS				$107.90		

SYSTEM PLAY VS REGULAR PLAY

2. THE ADDED FACTORS SYSTEM

Since reliable statistics show that about 35 percent or slightly more than a third of the favorites on the tote board come through as winners, the question naturally arises: "Which third?" Anyone with the absolute answer could fly south with the horses every winter, and go wherever else the bugle called, making a sure and steady profit at the tracks. Only soon there would be no tracks if it were just that simple.

However, there are ways that may help raise the winning average where actual races are concerned, and these come under the head of added factors, which accounts for the title of this system.

Using the popular choice, as indicated by the tote board's closing odds, the player simply decides whether or not he wants to ride along with the favorite or pass up the race entirely. To do this, he applies certain known factors to the many variables that have produced the favorite. In short, he checks to see if the choice is sound by his accepted standards. This requires a preliminary survey of the entries, along with some of their past records and present potentials, but these are all of a very obvious nature. No elaborate charts, exhaustive figuring or comparison of selections are needed. All you need to know are specific facts pertaining to the more likely horses in the races you intend to play. Then you—and they—are set to go.

The key to the situation is whether the chosen horse is a proven winner as well as a potential winner. It must have the class, form and condition to warrant your backing it in the current outing. This enables you to cross off certain races before you even reach the track. Those are: maiden races, which are run by horses that have never won a race and therefore don't figure; two-year-olds, which haven't been in business long enough to gain full rating; and also steeplechases, with their element of uncertainty, or any other events that you may regard as doubtful.

In the playable races, check any horses that rate as likely favorites. Figure these in terms of these three factors:

(A) PROVEN WINS

1. Give full rating to any horse that has a past record of one win in six races or better, as an overall average.
2. Give a half-rating to any horse that has gained a win in its last dozen tries.
3. Eliminate any horse with less wins.

(B) WINNING POTENTIAL

1. Give full rating to any horse that finished "in the money" in either of its last two races.
2. Give a half-rating to a horse that finished fourth or better in either of its last two starts.
3. Eliminate any horse that failed to run fourth or better in either of those races.
4. Recent races: Give a full rating to a horse that ran its last race within the past ten days.
5. Give a partial rating to a horse that ran its last race within the past two weeks.
6. Eliminate any horse that has not run within two weeks.

(C) NUMBER OF HORSES IN THE RACE

1. If there are less than ten horses entered in the race, a horse with two full ratings and one partial rating is worth a bet.
2. With ten horses or more, three full ratings are needed, one under each of the three main heads.

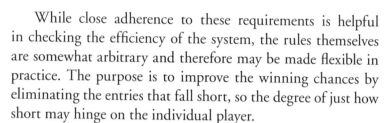

While close adherence to these requirements is helpful in checking the efficiency of the system, the rules themselves are somewhat arbitrary and therefore may be made flexible in practice. The purpose is to improve the winning chances by eliminating the entries that fall short, so the degree of just how short may hinge on the individual player.

Frequently, changing figures on the tote board may keep two entries practically equal choices as favorite, almost to the end. Hence it is good policy to make a comparative rating of likely favorites beforehand, so as to make a last-moment pick. Here, individual judgment is again the final factor.

Now let's look at a six-day chart, showing how these factors influenced the wagering on the tote board favorites.

SIX DAY CHART SHOWING INFLUENCE OF ADDED FACTORS

FIRST DAY

RACE	PROVEN WINS	LAST TWO FINISHES	PREVIOUS RACE	# OF ENTRIES	PLAYABLE OR NON-PLAYABLE	WIN	PLACE	SHOW
(1)	2 in 20	x-1	9 days	11	No play. Too few proven wins	X	X	X
(2)	1 in 18	3-2	15 days	11	No play. Too many days	X	X	X
(3)	1 in 17	3-1	7 days	12	No play. Too few wins	X	3.40	3.00
(4)	7 in 22	1-4	9 days	6	Playable	3.40	2.80	2.20
(5)					Non-Playable Type of Race	X	X	X
(6)	4 in 13	4-2	7 days	9	Playable	X	X	2.80
(7)	4 in 15	1-3	4 days	9	Playable	6.40	4.20	3.00
(8)	5 in 23	3-3	6 days	12	Playable	X	X	3.00
			Outlay on All Races:			$16.00 $9.80	$10.40	$14.00
			Outlay on Playable Races:			$8.00 $9.80	$7.00	$11.00

SEVEN SYSTEMS FOR PICKING WINNERS

RACE	PROVEN WINS	LAST TWO FINISHES	PREVIOUS RACE	# OF ENTRIES	PLAYABLE OR NON-PLAYABLE	WIN	PLACE	SHOW
SECOND DAY								
(1)					Non-Playable Type of Race	6.40	3.80	3.00
(2)	5 in 27	2-0	19 days	12	No play. Too many days lapse.	5.60	4.20	3.20
(3)a **b**	1 in 12 6 in 22	1-3 3-1	8 days 3 days	8	Too few wins. Playable, sufficient wins.	X 7.20	X 4.00	X 3.00
(4)a **b**	3 in 22 2 in 16	2-0 0-4	14 days 14 days	12 12	Neither playable. Weak on proven wins & days since previous race.	X X	X X	X X
(5)	4 in 19	1-1	5 days	12	Playable	3.00	2.80	2.60
(6)	2 in 23	3-4	12 days	10	No play. Too few wins. Too many days	X	X	X
(7)					Non-Playable Type of Race	X	X	X
(8)	2 in 11	3-3	9 days	11	Playable	X	X	3.40
Outlay on All Races:						**$16.00**	**$22.20**	**$14.80**	**$15.20**
Outlay on Playable Races:						**$6.00**	**$10.20**	**$6.80**	**$9.00**

RACE	PROVEN WINS	LAST TWO FINISHES	PREVIOUS RACE	# OF ENTRIES	PLAYABLE OR NON-PLAYABLE	WIN	PLACE	SHOW
THIRD DAY								
(1)					Non-Playable Type of Race	X	X	X
(2)	1 in 18	4-0	13 days	12	No play. Weak in all factors..	X	3.80	2.80
(3)					Non-Playable Type of Race.	X	X	2.80
(4)	None	4-4	11 days	12	No play.	X	X	X
(5)	None	0-2	4 days	12	No play.	X	X	X
(6)					Non-Playable Type of Race	X	X	X
(7)	5 in 26	0-2	13 days	9	Playable despite time lapse	X	X	X
(8)	2 in 11	3-3	9 days	11	Playable	X	X	3.40
Outlay on All Races:						**$16.00**	**$0.00**	**$3.80**	**$5.60**
Outlay on Playable Races:						**$2.00**	**$0.00**	**$0.00**	**$0.00**

RACE	PROVEN WINS	LAST TWO FINISHES	PREVIOUS RACE	# OF ENTRIES	PLAYABLE OR NON-PLAYABLE	WIN	PLACE	SHOW
					FOURTH DAY			
(1)					Non-Playable Type of Race	X	X	2.80
(2)	2 in 28	2-3	9 days	12	No play. Too few wins.	X	X	X
(3)	1 in last 12	3-3	9 days	6	Playable.	3.60	2.60	2.30
(4)					Non-Playable Type of Race	6.60	4.20	3.40
(5)	2 in 13	1-1	9 days	12	Playable with last 2 wins.	X	4.60	3.20
(6)	4 in 26	2-1	5 days	8	Playable	X	X	X
(7)	3 in 10	3-1	14 days	12	No play. Too many days.	X	X	X
(8)	1 in 14	4-2	5 days	12	No play. Too few wins.	X	3.00	2.80
					Outlay on All Races:	**$16.00**	**$10.20**	**$14.40**	**$14.50**
					Outlay on Playable Races:	**$4.00**	**$3.60**	**$2.60**	**$2.30**

RACE	PROVEN WINS	LAST TWO FINISHES	PREVIOUS RACE	# OF ENTRIES	PLAYABLE OR NON-PLAYABLE	WIN	PLACE	SHOW
					FIFTH DAY			
(1)	4 in 17	4-3	7 days	12	Playable	6.00	3.80	3.20
(2)	1 in 20	No wins	3 weeks	12	No play.	X	X	X
(3)	2 in 13	3-2	10 days	12	Just playable.	X	X	X
(4)					Non-Playable Type of Race	X	3.20	2.60
(5)	2 in 12	3-2	6 days	5	Playable.	5.00	2.80	2.20
(6)					Non-Playable Type of Race	X	X	X
(7)	5 in 14	x-3	6 days	9	Playable	6.80	3.80	3.40
(8)	2 in 13	x-2	3 weeks	12	No play.	X	X	X
					Outlay on All Races:	**$16.00**	**$17.80**	**$13.60**	**$11.40**
					Outlay on Playable Races:	**$8.00**	**$17.80**	**$13.60**	**$11.40**

					SIXTH DAY			
RACE	PROVEN WINS	LAST TWO FINISHES	PREVIOUS RACE	# OF ENTRIES	PLAYABLE OR NON-PLAYABLE	WIN	PLACE	SHOW
(1)					Non-Playable Type of Race	X	X	X
(2)	1 in 14	1-2	15 days	12	Non-Playable.	5.60	3.80	3.20
(3)	1 in 28	2-3	13 days	12	Non-Playable.	X	X	X
(4)	None	3-2	3 weeks	12	Non-Playable.	5.40	3.6	2.80
(5)					Non-Playable Type of Race.	5.20	3.60	3.00
(6)	4 in 24	2-2	10 days	9	Playable	6.40	3.20	2.80
(7)	2 in 11	3-3	5 days	10	Playable	X	4.80	3.00
(8)	4 in 16	3-1	8 days	12	Playable	8.40	4.20	3.60
					Outlay on All Races:	$16.00	$31.00	$23.20	$18.40
					Outlay on Playable Races:	$6.00	$17.80	$15.20	$11.60

		SIX-DAY TOTALS						
DAY	OUTLAY ON ALL RACES	RETURN			OUTLAY ON SYSTEM RACES	RETURN		
		WIN	PLACE	SHOW		WIN	PLACE	SHOW
1st	$16.00	9.80	10.40	14.00	8.00	9.80	7.00	11.00
2nd	16.00	22.20	14.80	15.20	6.00	10.20	6.80	9.00
3rd	16.00	0.00	3.80	3.00	2.00	0.00	0.00	0.00
4th	16.00	9.60	14.20	15.40	4.00	3.60	2.60	2.30
5th	16.00	17.80	13.60	11.40	8.00	17.80	13.60	11.40
6th	16.00	40.80	26.20	19.60	6.00	24.60	15.20	11.60
	96.00	100.20	93.00	78.60	34.00	66.00	45.20	45.30
		Profit $4.20	Loss $3.00	Loss $17.40		Profit $32.00	Profit $11.20	Profit $11.30

3. PLAYING THE FINAL RACE

Every racing day, so it is claimed, some quiet-mannered gentlemen go out to the nearest track long after the crowd has assembled there. They arrive in ample time to watch the tote board on the final race, usually the eighth, but at some tracks the ninth. Just before the windows close, these gentlemen show the only haste they have so far displayed, by heading to the $50 window and plunking a solid bet on the nose of the favorite registered on the tote board.

After that, they casually watch the race, wait until the crowd begins to thin, and then go to the pay-off windows to cash their winning tickets. There are days when they don't collect, because they do not expect to win more often than they would when playing any other horse that the public has made its favorite. But they are counting on a better return than usual, and according to rather reliable statistics, they should get it over the long run.

This system hinges on the recognized fact that the public generally overplays a favorite, thereby bringing the odds down below the profit level. The logical exception to this rule is the last race of the day, for the following reasons:

    a. Many of the small-time-favorite players have gone home, gone broke, or otherwise eliminated themselves from the betting before the last race is run.

    b. Conservative players who find themselves ahead are apt to take more of a chance on the last race, since they are betting some of their easy profits.

    c. Most losing players are inclined to aim for bigger odds in the final race, or even take a chance on a long shot in an effort to recoup their losses.

If any or all of these factors are at work, they keep the price up on the final favorite, thereby making its play profitable.

Whether or not the quiet-mannered gentlemen make a living from their application of such knowledge, it does seem that the average horseplayer would do well to consider the final race in terms of the favorite, rather than otherwise.

The examples that follow illustrate this point. All were taken from series of races run at different well-known tracks at about the same period. Each race represents the final event of the day stated. For convenience, the results and pay-offs are given on the basic scale of the familiar $2 bet, though it is customary to go heavier in such plays as these.

All bets are on a flat basis, the same amount being wagered on every race.

	TRACK A				TRACK B			
DAY	ODDS TO $1	STR.	PLACE	SHOW	ODDS TO $1	STR.	PLACE	SHOW
1	3.60	9.20	5.00	2.80	2.60	7.20	4.20	3.60
2	2.80	....	5.00	3.00	1.70	....	....	....
3	2.80	7.60	5.40	3.40	3.05	8.10	3.90	3.30
4	2.40	....	....	3.40	2.00	6.00	3.30	2.40
5	2.30	....	....	....	1.15	4.30	2.90	2.50
6	1.90	....	3.80	2.80	2.30	...	...	...
7	3.20	....	4.80	3.60	1.70	...	...	...
8	2.40	....	4.00	3.60	1.45	...	...	...
9	2.80	....	4.60	3.20	2.10	6.20	3.40	2.50
10	3.00	8.00	4.20	3.40	1.65	....	....	2.50
11	3.40	8.80	5.00	4.40	2.30	...	....	....
12	2.00	....	4.20	3.40	3.05	....	....	....
	Total $24.00	$33.60	$46.00	$37.00	Total $24.00	$31.80	$17.70	$16.80

| DAY | TRACK C | | | | TRACK D | | | |
	ODDS TO $1	STR.	PLACE	SHOW	ODDS TO $1	STR.	PLACE	SHOW
1	2.30	6.60	3.20	2.60	2.40	6.80	3.60	2.80
2	4.10	....	....	....	3.60	....	....	....
3	1.50	....	3.00	2.40	1.30	....	3.20	2.60
4	3.60	....	....	....	3.00	8.00	4.60	3.20
5	3.30	....	....	....	2.50	....	....	3.20
6	2.30	6.60	4.00	3.40	2.30	....	4.20	2.80
	Total $12.00	$13.20	$10.20	$8.40	Total $12.00	$14.80	$15.60	$14.60

The question of whether to play these final races straight, place, show, or in combination resolves itself into two logical answers, each representing a different type of wager:

1. Since the player is anticipating an average percentage of wins, but is counting on higher odds, he should consider straight bets only. If the horses run true to form, his return should be above the profit level.

2. The fact that the odds run higher than average may leave doubt as to the actual favorite in a race, as the nearest contender may be bet down to the favorite's price. By betting the horse to place, the player allows for this; and if his choice is nosed out by the true favorite, he still has a winner.

At tracks where the favorites in the last race are well defined and apparently consistent, straight bets may be in order; but as a general run, the place method is preferable. Switching from one mode of play to the other is not advisable, as a few wrong guesses may throw both out of line.

Note that in the group of races listed, the results from straight and place play are reasonably close, the returns from a $72 investment being $93.40 on straight bets and $89.50 on place bets. Show bets only brought a return of $76.80, which is why they are not considered in this system. On a $20 play per race, this would bring a net profit of $214 on straight bets, or $175 on place bets, but since only one race is a day, the average profit over the series of thirty-six races would be only $5 or $6 a day.

Since that would no more than pay for the trip out to the track, most players may prefer to use the last-race method simply as a booster for some other system. Anyone hoping to use it as a steady earner would have to back it to the tune of $100 a play or more. This is the biggest reason why a player should forego straight bets and back each horse to place. He might be sunk if he ran into a string of straight losses at the very outset, whereas the greater frequency of place pay-offs is some insurance against such misfortune.

Quite often, this type of play will come through in a most gratifying style. Here, for example, is a list of twelve races, taken from different tracks over a period of a few days, all representing the favorite in the final race:

FINAL RACE FAVORITE				
RACE	BET	STRAIGHT	PLACE	SHOW
1	$2	...	.....	...
2	2	$7.80	$4.20	$3.20
3	2	7.10	4.10	3.10
4	2	.....	3.20	2.80
5	2	4.40	2.80	2.40
6	2	.....	3.60	2.70
7	2	7.20	5.00	3.60
8	2	4.00	3.00	2.20
9	2	5.20	3.20	2.60
10	2	4.30	2.70	2.10
11	2	.....	5.20	3.20
12	2	.....	.....	...
Total	$24	$40.00	$37.00	$27.90

4. THE QUICK REPEAT SYSTEM

When a favorite romps home a winner, it represents a horse that has reached its peak of form. That, at least, is the opinion of the majority of those who backed it; otherwise they would not have backed it so heavily. It also marks the horse as a proper play by the "quick repeat" system. Opinions differ on whether a horse should be played again, following a win. Some players feel that it may have passed its peak. Others don't like to risk their money on the same nag, figuring they may pay back some solid cash they should have been smart enough to keep. This is particularly true after winning on a low-odds choice.

Many players may be disappointed by the low "take" and, therefore, be all the more anxious to hang on to what they made. They may even figure that the profit wasn't worth the play. With the horse thus pegged in their minds, they are all the more likely to lay off it the next time it runs.

That's where the system player comes in. From the day a track opens, he should keep a careful check of all horses that came in winners at the lowest odds in the race. That last point is all-important. An ordinary winner won't do. It is apt to attract more bettors than it loses, when it runs again.

But the winning favorite is a different story and one that may have a happy ending. Proponents of this system bet on such a horse to repeat, believing that its chances will be as good as in its winning race and that the odds are likely to be higher. The player can allow for any falloff in the horses form by betting it to place and show in whatever proportions he prefers.

Now for some additional angles, which are conducive of some longer odds. In full, the rules run:

1. Watch for winning favorites and back such a horse in its next race, on the chance it will repeat.

2. Also watch for favorites that run second and play them to repeat. Simply make sure that such a horse ran a good second or staged a strong finish. This classes it as a potential winner.

3. When a horse fails to repeat, play it in one more race, provided it runs within a ten-day period. This indicates the horse is still in form and worth another play.

4. If a horse wins, play it in its next race. Keep after those repeats; and the bigger the odds, the better.

5. If a horse finishes in the money (second or third), play it for another repeat, provided it ran at low odds and preferably as favorite. Here, the odds show sharpness.

6. The next race should be run within ten days or two weeks of the horse's previous try, though some players allow more leeway for a similar type of race at the same track.

When heavy betting cuts the odds, it at least indicates a horse's merit. That gives you all the more reason to stay along with the same horse on another repeat.

Now let's look at some case histories, starting with a horse called Mostest.

MOSTEST

Mostest qualified for play by running second at odds of approximately 3 to 2, paying $3.10 to place, $2.60 to show. In subsequent races, this horse ran:

MOSTEST			
	STRAIGHT	PLACE	SHOW
2nd (as odds-on favorite)	....	3.10	2.60
2nd (as odds-on favorite)	....	3.00	2.40
1st (as coupled entry)	$3.00	2.60	2.20
1st (as odds-on favorite)	2.80	2.50	2.30
4th (at approx. 3 to 1)	....	....	....
	$5.80	$11.20	$9.50

This was not a profitable sequence and it represents the low priced type of play that this system is usually able to avoid, as in the case of Matizar.

MATIZAR

Matizar began by winning a race as favorite and paying $6.60 straight, $3.80 to place, and $2.90 to show. In subsequent races this horse ran as follows:

MATIZAR			
	STRAIGHT	PLACE	SHOW
2nd (at 4.70 to 1)	...	4.50	2.70
1st favorite	8.10	4.10	2.90
2nd (at 5.5 to 1)	...	6.00	4.50
1st (12.45 to 1)	26.90	8.30	5.20
1st (at 2.35 to 1)	6.70	3.10	2.50
6th (at approx. 3 to 1)	....	....	....
	$41.70	$26.00	$17.80

After its one dismal fizzle, this horse remained idle over a period of more than two weeks, eliminating it from further consideration in this series. Let's look at the next horse.

TOMAN

Toman qualified by winning as favorite at odds of 3 to 2, paying $5 straight, $3.50 to place, and $3.10 to show. It then ran:

TOMAN			
	STRAIGHT	PLACE	SHOW
1st (at approx. 3 to 2) favorite	$5.10	$3.90	$3.00
3rd (at approx. 3 to 1) favorite	....	....	2.80
2nd (under 2 to 1) coupled entry	....	3.00	2.70
1st (at 3 to 2) favorite	5.00	3.30	2.50
8th (at 2.10 to 1) coupled entry	....	....	....
	$10.10	$10.20	$11.00

After that failure, the horse did not run for more than ten days. It ran at a different track some two weeks later, which marked it as unplayable. It came in tenth.

This example brings up the question of playing a coupled entry. The answer is: With this system, yes. Experienced players regard a two-horse deal as a bargain, and since we're banking on a repeat, so much the better. As an interesting illustration, take a look at Jet Black.

JET BLACK

Jet Black won as the favorite at slightly over 2 to 1, paying $6.90 straight, $3.90 to place, and $2.90 to show. In the following races, the horse ran:

JET BLACK			
	STRAIGHT	PLACE	SHOW
3rd (at 2.25 to 1) coupled entry	....	$4.30	$4.30
2nd (approx. 6 to 1) coupled entry	....	5.50	4.00
2nd (3.60 to 1) almost favorite	....	4.10	2.70
1st (4.35 to 1)	$10.70	5.00	3.70
4th (5.25 to 1)	....	....	....
	$10.70	$18.90	$14.70

This would have been worth another play on the chance of a rebound, but the horse did not run for a month, which ended the sequence. This raises a moot question, as with our next horse, On To Victory.

ON TO VICTORY

On to Victory ran as the favorite, winning and paying $5.70 straight, $3.30 to place, and $2.50 to show. It then ran:

JET BLACK			
	STRAIGHT	PLACE	SHOW
4th (at approx. 5 to 1)	....	....	...
3rd (at 1.35 to 1) favorite	....	....	2.80
1st (at nearly 12 to 1)	25.40	11.10	6.70
1st* (over 7 to 1)	16.40	5.70	4.00
3rd* (over 9 to 1)	....	....	2.80
2nd* (at 2.05 to 1) favorite	....	4.00	3.30
6th (at 2.60 to 1) favorite	...	...	...
	$41.80	$20.80	$19.60

Due to a time lapse of more than two weeks between the two winning races, some players might have eliminated the three starred (*) races. But the second win was gained at the same track, under the same conditions, at slightly less distance and against horses that had taken a longer layoff. The promise of high odds also warranted another play after a spectacular win.

Here are some examples of shorter sequences that stemmed from races where the horses ran as favorites and finished first or second:

FAVORITES FINISHING 1ST OR 2ND			
	STRAIGHT	**PLACE**	**SHOW**
Horse A	....	$2.70	$2.60
	...	4.90	3.50
	....	....	...
Horse B	....	4.10	3.40
	...	3.70	2.70
	....	....	...
Horse C	$3.10	2.70	2.20
	5.50	3.30	2.70
	3.00	2.70	2.30
Horse D	....	4.20	3.20
	...	7.80	4.80
Horse E	....	....	2.60
	$11.60	$36.10	$30.00

These shorter runs are generally unprofitable as they include horses that are dropping off in form and seldom bring high odds. But they are needed to build the longer sequences that offer bigger return.

Added to the sequences given earlier, the total came to:

SUMMARY				
# OF RACES	STRAIGHT	PLACE	SHOW	AMOUNT ON EACH
41 Races at $2	$121.70	$123.30	$102.60	$84.00
Across the Board: $347.60 return from a play of $252.00				

5. THE BEST OF FOUR SYSTEM

Figures on favorites indicate that as odds drop, the percentage of wins rises, but the pay-off still remains too low in proportion. Since the odds cannot be changed, the problem is to eliminate the least likely winners by passing up such races. In every race, certain horses are dangerous where the favorite's chances are concerned. The fewer such horses the better, which is the sole basis for the present system. The favorite must be the best of four potential winners—and no more. Otherwise the race is ignored.

Now as to what constitutes a potential winner. This is somewhat arbitrary and varies in many races and at different tracks, but for a working basis, odds of 10 to 1 can be taken as the line of demarcation. Once a horse's odds drop below that, he can be considered dangerous.

So you simply watch the totalizer and keep count of how many horses flash below 10 to 1. If there are no more than four, your bet is the horse with the lowest odds, namely the tote board favorite. But let more than four drop below that 10 to 1 margin and there is no play.

Sometimes, of course, you will have to add a dash of your own mental judgment, along with the physical dash that you must make to the betting window before it closes. If two horses are too close a choice for favorite, pass up the race rather than guess wrong on a straight bet. If odds on a fifth horse threaten to drop below 10 to 1, pass up the race. Count coupled entries as individual horses, as they are just that many more entries for yours to beat. Do not back a coupled entry unless it is a very solid favorite.

As illustration, take the results of these three first-day races at a popular Eastern track.

BEST OF FOUR SYSTEM								
RACE 1			RACE 2			RACE 3		
HORSE	ODDS TO $1	FINISH	HORSE	ODDS TO $1	FINISH	HORSE	ODDS TO $1	FINISH
A	$1.20	1	AA	$6.60	1	AAA	$1.70	c-1
B	4.80	2	BB	4.30	2	BBB	1.90	2
C	16.00	3	CC	3.50	3	CCC	4.20	3
D	57.40	4	DD	21.20	4	DDD	61.20	4
E	3.90	5	EE	2.40	5	EEE	6.80	5
F	14.90	6	FF	54.00	6	FFF	12.00	6
G	12.80	7	GG	79.10	7	GGG	1.70	c-7
H	63.00	8	HH	4.10	e-8			
I	25.10	9	II	4.10	e-9			
J	91.60	10	JJ	107.80	10			
K	185.50	11	KK	377.50	11			
L	82.90	12						

In Race 1, the favorite was well defined, with only two challengers, three horses in all, under the 10 to 1 mark. The favorite, Horse A, came through as expected, paying $4.40 on a $2 ticket. The fantastic odds on many of the horses indicated that they should hardly have been considered in the race. Horse A was a good example of a playable favorite, by this system.

In Race 2, too many horses were under 10 to 1, six in all, counting HH and II separately, though they were an entry (as indicated by "e"). The favorite, EE, was shaded closely by the next best choice, CC, leaving doubt up to the last moment as to which to pick. An utterly unplayable race, which was passed.

In Race 3, there were five horses under 10 to 1, making it unplayable. The low odds of the entry (AAA and GGG) and the next choice (BBB) made it impossible to pick a favorite.

Using this pattern of play, a series of fifty races produced twenty-four winners, a 48 percent average, at the track mentioned, during a two-week meeting. These showed a profit on a flat bet basis, which included odds-on favorites, horses running at less than even money.

6. THE PROGRESSIVE PLAY SYSTEM

Such a high percentage offers opportunities for a progressive or cumulative betting system, so with the tabulated results are included the figures on a "slow" system and a "steep" system. In the slow, or gradual form of wagering, the odds-on horses are eliminated, because they do not give the player a sufficient cash return.

But with the steep system, small wins are important, so the odds-on favorites are included in the play. Other comments on betting methods follow the tabulation and should be duly noted.

SEVEN SYSTEMS FOR PICKING WINNERS

FIFTY-RACE CHART

| RACE | FLAT BETS | | | PROGRESSIVES | | | |
| | STRAIGHT | PLACE | SHOW | SLOW | | STEEP | |
				BET	RETURN	BET	RETURN
1	$4.40	$2.80	$2.60	$2	$4.40	$2	$4.40
2	4.40	3.60	2.80	2	4.40	2	4.40
3	3.80	2.80	2.40	2	3.80	2	3.80
4	5.40	2.60	2.20	2	5.40	2	5.40
5	....	....	....	2	....	2	...
6				2	....	4	....
7	5.40	3.00	2.40	4	10.80	12	32.40
8	4.20	3.00	2.20	2	4.20	2	4.20
9	....	....	....	(No play)	2	....	
10			2.60	2	...	4	....
11		2.20	2.20	(No play)	12	....	
12		3.60	2.80	2	....	36	....
13		3.60	2.60	4	....	2	....
14	....	....	3.40	6	....	4	....
15	6.80	3.60	2.60	10	34.00	12	40.80
16	4.60	3.40	2.60	2	4.60	2	4.60
17	4.40	3.00	3.20	2	4.40	2	4.40
18	3.40	3.00	2.60	(No play)	2	3.40	
19	2.80	2.40	2.20	(No play)	2	2.80	
20	....	....	....	2	....	2	....
21	....	....	....	2	....	4	....
22	5.40	3.80	2.60	4	10.80	12	32.40
23	5.80	4.00	3.20	2	5.80	2	5.80
24	....	2.80	2.40	2	....	2	....
25	....	....	...	$2	...	$4	....
26	$5.00	$2.80	$2.60	4	$10.00	12	$30.00
27	....	2.80	2.60	2	...	2	....
28	....	3.40	2.80	(No play)	4	....	
29	4.60	3.00	2.70	2	4.60	12	27.60
30	....	....	....	2	....	2	....
31	...	3.00	2.20	(No play)	2	3.40	
32	....	....	....	2	....	12	....
33	....	3.80	3.20	4	....	36	....
34	....	4.80	5.00	6	....	2	....
35	....	....	3.40	10	....	4	....
36	4.20	3.00	2.80	16	33.60	12	25.20
37	7.00	4.00	3.20	2	7.00	2	7.00
38	....	....	....	2	....	2	....
39	4.60	3.00	2.80	2	4.60	4	9.20
40	4.80	2.80	2.60	2	4.80	2	4.80
41	3.40	2.20	2.20	(No play)	2	3.40	
42	3.60	2.80	2.40	(No play)	2	3.60	
43	....	4.40	2.80	2	....	2	....
44	5.80	3.80	3.40	2	5.80	4	11.60
45	....	....	....	2	....	2	....
46	....	3.20	2.80	2	....	4	...
47	6.60	3.40	2.60	4	13.20	12	39.60
48	....	4.40	2.80	2	....	2	....
49	5.80	3.80	3.40	2	5.80	4	11.60
50	....	3.20	2.80	2	....	2	....
$100	$116.20	$120.80	$110.70	$134	$182	$282	$322.40
Profit:	$16.20	$20.80	$10.70		$48.00		$40.40

THE SLOW PROGRESSION PROCESS

The **slow progression** used was the 2, 2, 4, 6, 10, 16. It did not go beyond that many plays, which was within the limit of expected profit. For example, if a play had been made on the thirty-first race, $16 would have been lost on the thirty-fifth race, making a total of $40 loss on that series (races 30-35 inclusive).

If the player had taken that loss, he would have wagered only $2 on the thirty-sixth race, for a return of $4.20 (instead of $16 for a return of $33.60), which would have cut his profit by another $15.40. This would have reduced $48 profit over the entire group of races to a loss of $7.40.

However, where "ifs" are concerned, the player should, and might, have passed the thirty-sixth race, which was very close to being an odds-on affair; in fact, anything below 1.60 to 1 is dubious; and this was a 1.10 to 1 play. So, if he had passed both the thirty-first and thirty-sixth races, his $16 on the thirty-seventh race would have brought home a rousing $56.

Profits of $17.60 and $5 on the thirty-sixth and thirty-seventh races would have become $40 profit on the thirty-seventh race alone, giving the player $17.60 more on the overall play, or a total profit of $65.60 instead of $48.

THE STEEP PROGRESSION PROCESS

The **steep progression** was the type that doubled all previous totals (2, 4, 12, 36) and quit after the fourth loss in the series, taking a $54 loss. This, of course, included odds-on horses, and though it ran out twice, it still brought a $38.40 profit. But it required more capital than the slow system, with greater risk.

There are certain ways of tightening this system that are especially helpful in progressive play. One is to pass all races in which more than half the horses are under 10 to 1. Specifically, this would eliminate those in which four horses are under 10 to 1, with seven horses in the race; and events with three horses under 10 to 1, with only five steeds running.

In the chart given, this would have eliminated the fourth, eighth, tenth, eleventh and twenty-fifth races. That might have saved the player $40 in the steep progression, as the thirteenth race was somewhat doubtful, so six successive losses (races 9-14 inclusive) could have been reduced to three through tight play. Added to those restrictions is an even stronger one, namely to gear the play to the "best of three" instead of the "best of four." This tends to boost the percentage of wins, but it reduces the number of playable races almost to the vanishing point at some tracks.

This can be tempered by starting out with the "best of four," and applying the "best of three" after the first losing race in a sequence, then using the "best of four" again, following the next win. This is continued throughout, wherever a progression is utilized.

At some tracks, it is better to use the "best of four" system throughout in order to get sufficient action, but to eliminate all races with more than ten horses, or even those with more than eight, as the added nags may include sleepers above 10 to 1, thus hampering the system.

7. THE FOUR FOR FOUR SYSTEM

This simple but intriguing system is based on statistics showing that post-time favorites are the winners in approximately one-third of the races run at most tracks. That being the case, extended losing streaks of more than four races cannot be too common, or the average would not stay up.

So the player simply follows the favorites, and whenever they have lost four races in a row, he bets on the next race and keeps on betting until he hits a winner. That gained, he sits back and waits for four more successive losers before he makes another bet on a favorite.

Incidentally, statistics indicate that such a win should usually bring a better than average price because, although a winner is overdue, the public begins to become dubious about backing favorites after four or more losses. Also, some conservative players have to jump to higher odds brackets to recoup their losses. So, the man who waits has an edge.

Now, if simply played race by race, carrying over day by day, this system would be badly lacking in that thing called action. A player might not make a bet in a week or more. So to punch it up, the player also keeps track of the day's races by number: first race, second race, and so on. When any such race shows losses for four successive days, the player backs the favorite in that race on the next day, and so on, until he wins.

A study of the following chart explains this, with "W" representing winning favorites and "L" the losing favorites in races that were *not* played. In the races that were played, a win is indicated by the return on a $2 ticket, a loss by the word "Lost."

Day	1st	2nd	3rd	4th	5th	6th	7th	8th
FOUR FOR FOUR SYSTEM RACE RESULTS								
1	W	L	W	L	L	W	L	L
2	L	L	Lost	Lost	$6.60	W	W	L
3	W	L	W	L	L	W	W	W
4	W	W	W	L	L	L	L	$5.50
5	W	L	L	Lost	L	$4.70	L	L
6	L	W	W	Lost	W	W	W	L
7	L	L	L	*	Lost	Lost	$6.20	W
8	W	W	L	$4.20	L	W	W	W
9	L	L	L	W	L	L	L	L
10	Lost	Lost	$2.90	L	L	W	W	L
11	W	W	L	W	5.10	L	L	W
12	L	L	L	W	L	W	L	L
13	L	L	7.00	L	L	L	W	L
14	W	L	L	L	L	5.30	L	L
15	L	L	8.80	L	L	W	W	W
16	L	$4.40	W	L	Lost	L	L	Lost
17	$3.20	W	L	Lost	Lost	L	Lost	4.60
18	L	W	L	Lost	4.80	L	L	W
19	W	W	L	Lost	L	W	W	L
20	L	L	W	Lost	W	L	W	L
21	W	L	L	Lost	W	W	L	L
22	W	L	L	Lost	L	4.10	L	L
23	W	L	L	Lost	W	W	W	Lost
24	L	Lost	W	5.80	L	L	L	Lost
25	7.60	5.50	W	W	L	L	L	Lost
26	5.00	W	L	L	W	L	W	W
27	L	L	L	L	6.50	W	L	L
28	L	L	5.90	W	L	L	L	L
29	Lost	Lost	3.00	W	L	L	W	L
30	L	W	W	L	L	L	W	L
31	7.50	W	L	L	L	L	Lost	6.40
32	W	L	L	L	3.80	Lost	W	L
33	W	L	L	L	L	Lost	5.10	L
34	W	W	L	Lost	L	4.20	W	L
35	L	L	Lost	4.10	L	L	*	L
36	L	8.80	3.30	L	L	W	L	7.50
37	L	L	W	W	Lost	W	L	L
38	L	W	L	L	3.40	L	L	W
39	5.60	L	L	L	L	Lost	7.10	L
40	L	L	W	W	L	W	*	W
41	L	W	L	L	L	W	L	L
42	L	L	Lost	Lost	5.30	L	L	W
43	L	L	L	L	5.10	L	W	L
44	3.30	W	L	W	L	L	L	W

Total Number of Races Played: 71 at $2, for $142
Total Number of Wins: 37, with return of $197.20
Profit from Play at $2: $55.20
On Basis of $10 Flat Bet: $261.00

ANALYZING THE FOUR FOR FOUR CHART

Favorites lost in the seventh and eighth races on the first day and in the first and second races on the second day. That made four in a row, so the player bet on the favorite in the next race. Two such races (the third and fourth) were "Lost," while a win in the next (fifth) race brought a return of $6.60 and ended that sequence of play.

On the fourth day, four consecutive losers in the fourth, fifth, sixth and seventh races called for a play in the eighth race that resulted in a $5.50 win, ending that sequence.

Beginning with the fifth day, the player had to keep tabs on the vertical columns as well as the cross row. The fourth-race column, with four consecutive losses, called for a play on which the player "Lost," as indicated, keeping that column open for a play the next day. Meanwhile, four consecutive losses on the fifth day (in the second, third, fourth and fifth races) demanded a play (in the sixth race) that resulted in a $4.70 win, ending that cross sequence.

Run through the entire chart and wherever you see four losses ("L" or "Lost") in any row, across or down, you will find a play registered in the next race. The only exceptions are a few races marked with an asterisk (*), in which the odds on the favorite were so low that a play was inadvisable. Any such races were simply eliminated and did not count either as a win or a loss. Any losing sequence was continued in such cases.

A study of the chart shows that although the total wins were less than 40 per cent of all the races run, the number of wins was slightly above 50 per cent in the races actually played. So in this case, it turned out as expected with a tidy profit as indicated.

Use of the system on a basis of individual races, as indicated by the vertical columns, is justified because statistics show that percentages of winning favorites stay fairly close to average expectancy when calculated in terms of first, second, third race and so on. So with all those columns working, the player gets the action that would otherwise be absent.

One apparent weakness in this system is the chance of hitting long strings of losers even though they should not normally occur. But this is not as serious as it seems. A series of more than twelve consecutive losses is rare at any track and the player would not be wavering on the first four. In fact, the chart shows a series of eleven straight losses in the fourth-race column, which on a $2 basis meant an expenditure of $16 to get back $5.80 on the next play. But that was offset by the other sequences in which the "hits" came sooner.

However, as a safeguard or insurance, a player can block off a sequence after seven straight losses, ignoring it until after a win. This means a total loss of three plays only. In this case it would have saved the player $4.20, namely $10 on five races less the $5.80 that the sixth brought in.

Critics are quick to discount systems based on the theory that the longer a string of losses, the more chance of a win. Such criticism is sound in the tossing of a coin, where the chance of a head or tail is still an even gamble, even if a dozen heads have just been tossed in a row. The same applies to red or black in roulette. Each spin of the wheel is a law unto itself.

But there, inanimate objects are involved. In racing, the element that keeps the winning favorites within an average range is the mood of the players. When post-time favorites are losing, it may be that too many bettors are backing the wrong horse and setting up a false favorite as a result. Consecutive losses tend to rectify that situation, enabling the smart player to cash in when the betting becomes more sound.

That, at least, is the theory behind the "four for four" system, though how well it works in practice is something to be tested and is apt to vary according to certain tracks. It can be worked on a basis of "five for five" if you prefer, making plays after five straight losses instead of only four. That tends to lessen your losses, but it also lessens your action, which means less wins. The same applies even more so in a "six for six."

One suggested use for the "four for four" is as a supplementary form of betting when visiting the same track day by day, as it then can be operated on a bonus basis without overworking it.

The next chapter outlines betting systems based on middle odds and overlays.

7 MIDDLE ODDS AND OVERLAYS

The wagering systems presented in this chapter are based on middle odds and overlays. **Middle odds** refers to horses with odds that are above 2 to 1 (the favorite) and below 6 to 1 (the long shot). An **overlay** refers to a horse whose odds of winning are high when compared with its winning chances.

Following are six powerful plays.

1. THE COUPLED ENTRY ANGLE

One of the bargain attractions of the racing business is the **coupled entry**, in which two horses from the same stable are entered as a team, so that money wagered on either horse applies to both. Many racing fans go after this bargain basement proposition and, appropriately, enough find themselves in the basement along with the bargain horses! On other occasions, the entry pays off, which leaves a player in an unhappy mood for not riding along with it.

So the question is: "When should you play and when should you *not* play a coupled entry?"

With certain systems, the entry can be played exactly like a single horse, the "bargain" angle being helpful. With others, it is better to pass up the race entirely, rather than throw the system out of gear. But we are dealing now with the coupled entry as a play in its own right.

Should you grab this chance if it comes along? The answer is yes—if the angle looks right. Summed up in simple terms, the coupled entry offers three distinct possibilities:

1. A chance to play two likely winners.
2. A chance to play a likely winner and a probable loser.
3. A chance to play two almost certain losers.

Analyzed, the first possibility is as good a bet as anyone would want. So good, in fact, that it's worth risking the second possibility. Rather than miss two likely winners, go along with a winner and a loser. But dodge the third prospect, that of two losers. Generally, the odds will tell; therefore, they are as good a guide as any. If smart players see an opportunity and latch on to it, the dropping odds should indicate that one horse or the other has a good chance and perhaps both. The odds are apt to be right when they drop below 7 to 1.

In some cases, a horse begins to lose the character of a long shot when its odds work down into the broad belt between 5 to 1 and 15 to 1. It may prove to be an overlay on the simple possibility that it was overlooked. But a coupled entry never is overlooked.

Some players just can't resist betting on two horses for the price of one even if the pair is sure to finish ninth and tenth in a ten-horse race. So the entry is bound to get a play that gives a false notion of its worth. But if it comes down too far, you can be sure that the long-shot players aren't trying to kill their own odds. Some new and more solid element has entered.

There are various angles with coupled entries. Perhaps one horse is ready for a win, while the other just needs exercise. Possibly one may gain needed confidence by seeing its stable mate go to the post with it. Maybe the owner wants to find which of his two horses is better. Add any more reasons that you want and if they total 6 to 1 or more, forget them and the horses with them.

The following chart gives some figures on such races, covering coupled entries just as they came along at different tracks, but all at the same period.

RACE	NO. OF HORSES	HOW ENTRY FINISHED	ODDS TO $1	STR.	PLACE	SHOW
TRACK ONE						
1	14	1st and 11th	$5.10	$12.20	$6.20	$3.80
2	9	3rd and 7th	2.70	....	....	2.40
3	14	6th and 7th	4.00	....	....	....
4	12	1st and 10th	2.30	6.60	4.00	3.20
5*	9	1st and 9th	9.00	20.00	9.20	5.00
6	9	7th and 9th	5.10	....	....	...
7	8	1st and 4th	.90	3.80	2.70	2. 0
8	14	1st and 2nd	3.20	8.40	8.20	5.30
9	12	5th and 10th	1.80	...	...	...
10	9	1st and 4th	1.60	5.00	3.10	2.30
11*	9	7th and 8th	7.75	....	....	....
12*	11	6th and 11th	6.90	....	....	....
13	8	3rd and 5th	1.00	....	....	2.20
14*	9	6th and 8th	13.15	....	....	....
15	9	5th and 6th	2.20	....	....	...
16	9	5th and 9th	4.70	....	...	...
17*	10	2nd and 10th	26.30	....	17.40	8.00
18	10	3rd and 4th	6.20	. ..	....	3.80
19	14	lst and 6th	1.95	5.90	3.50	2.90
20	7	4th and 5th	2.20	...	...	...
21	9	2nd and 3rd	2.20	...	2.80	3.60
22	11	1st and 7th	.40	2.80	2.20	2.20
23a	8	2nd and 4th	2.30	....	2.80	2.40
23b	8	1st and 6th	1.60	5.20	2.60	2.20
24*	10	5th and 9th	14.70	....	....	....
25	8	1st and 8th	1.20	4.40	3.20	2.60
26	8	1st and 4th	4.35	10.70	5.20	3.10
27 Plays at $54.00 All Plays				$85.20	$73.10	$57.40
21 Plays at $42				$65.20	$55.70	$44.40

Listings "a" and "b" under Race 23 represent two coupled entries. Both were played, so that there were four horses out of eight that might have finished in the money, and two did. Eliminating long shots (7 to 1 and over) did not improve the earnings, as Races 5 and 17 showed big returns.

However, the more conservative play proved profitable. Its value is more emphasized by the following series of plays at one track over a two-week period.

RACE	NO. OF HORSES	HOW ENTRY FINISHED	ODDS TO $1	STR.	PLACE	SHOW
TRACK TWO						
1a	11	1st and 9th	$1.20	$4.40	$2-90	$2.30
1b*	11	3rd and 8th	17.35	....	....	4.80
2	7	1st and 6th	3.75	9.50	3.80	3.40
3*	9	1st and 6th	7.85	17.70	6.40	4.10
4*	14	8th and 9th	56.75	....	....	....
5*	11	5th and 9th	8.25	....	....	....
6*	12	3rd and 11th	25.20	....	....	10.20
7*	10	5th and 6th	7.80	....	....	....
8*	11	5th and 8th	18.35	....	....	....
9a	14	1st and 3rd	5.10	12.20	5.40	7.20
9b	14	2nd and 6th	3.45	....	4.40	4.20
10	7	1st and 6th	3.05	8.10	3.80	2.30
11a*	16	6th and 11th	12.20	....	....	....
11b*	16	10th and 15th	10.80	....	....	....
12	7	3rd and 5th	3.55	....	....	....
13	7	1st and 5th	1.55	5.10	3.10	2.60
14	7	4th and 6th	11.50	....	....	....
15*	17	11th and 16th	37.35	....	....	....
16*	17	16th and 17th	25.05	....	...	...
17a*	14	2nd and 13th	36.80	....	19.30	12.00
17b	14	4th and 12th	2.05	....	....	....
18*	12	9th and 12th	14.20	....	....	....
19	10	4th and 5th	2.70	....	....	. ..
20	6	1st and 5th	3.55	9.10	4.10	2.80
21	14	3rd and 11th	4.05	...	...	3.60
22	9	1st and 3rd	4.55	11.10	4.60	5.40
23	13	4th and 9th	3.00	....	...	...
24	9	2nd and 9th	3.15	....	2.70	2.50
25	7	5th and 6th	2.40	....	...	....
26	8	1st and 7th	6.10	14.20	5.50	4.50
30 Plays at $60.00 All Plays				$91.40	$66.00	$71.00
17 Plays at $34 (All under 7 to 1)				$73.70	$40.30	$40.80

Here, a play on every coupled entry brought $3 for each $2 invested in straight bets, while place and show produced a slight profit. But the conservative play (under 7 to 1) did much better, more than doubling the return on straight bets, and doing a little better as to percentage on both place and show.

But the big factor is the way in which the straight bets came through, beginning with three in a row (4.40, 9.50, 12.20) in return for $6 wagered, with only one loss (Race 9b) before the next win (Race 10). The player built $26 into a return of $59.50 (at the end of Race 22) before encountering three losses in a row (Races 23, 24, 25), only to get back the expenditure ($6) with a win on the last race ($14.20), which added to the profit.

Here is another series of results from a different track, representing a three-week play of coupled entries.

RACE	NO. OF HORSES	HOW ENTRY FINISHED	ODDS TO $1	STR.	PLACE	SHOW
1	9	2nd and 3rd	$4.00	....	$4.20	$4.30
2	9	1st and 3rd	.90	$3.80	2.40	2.50
3	10	3rd and 4th	3.20	....	....	3.00
4	7	2nd and 3rd	1.80	....	2.70	2.80
5*	9	5th and 8th	35.35	....	....	....
6	10	6th and 9th	3.00	....	....	....
7	9	3rd and 7th	1.00	...	...	2.20
8	8	1st and 7th	6.35	14.70	7.00	4.40
9	8	3rd and 4th	2.65	...	...	2.80
10	7	1st and 3rd	7.20	16.40	3.80	4.00
11*	8	4th and 5th	9.20	....	....	....
12	7	1st and 3rd	1.05	4.10	2.60	2.70
13a	12	1st and 10th	3.40	8.80	4.70	3.30
13b	12	3rd and 9th	1.55	....	....	2.80
14	9	1st and 4th	1.75	5.50	3.30	2.60
15	8	6th and 7th	3.50	....	....	...
16	9	3rd and 6th	2.95	....	....	2.30
17a	9	1st and 7th	6.15	14.30	6.10	3.60
17b*	9	5th and 6th	10.80	....	....	....
18	9	1st and 8th	2.45	6.90	4.10	3.30
19	8	3rd and 4th	1.40	...	....	2.30
20a	11	1st and 4th	5.25	12.50	5.80	3.70
20b*	11	2nd and 5th	10.05	....	7.60	4.60
20c	11	3rd and 7th	1.95	....	....	2.90
20d*	11	10th and 11th	16.45	....	....	....
25 Plays at $50.00 All Plays				$87.00	$54.30	$60.10
20 Plays at $40				$87.00	$46.70	$55.50

2. THE SELECTIVE PLACE SYSTEM

The big problem in backing a selector's choice for a winner is that too many other players do the same, bringing down the odds on that particular horse, not only on straight bets, but on place and show as well. Normally, the general tendency to spread the bets brings them below the profitable level, whatever the type of wager.

Betting the selector's second choice instead of his first has a similar disadvantage. Returns may be higher per race, but the horses win less frequently. A **second favorite**, as such a horse is styled, receives its due proportion of the general play, and is apt to suffer accordingly, along with the player. It may be more or less per race, but the player loses in the long run.

There is one angle generally overlooked where the "second choice" is concerned; namely, that it may not be the selector's idea of an alternate winner, but his actual pick as the runner-up. Some races may be a tossup when it comes to a selection, but there are others where one horse is a standout, and the best of the rest is simply a placer due to finish second.

In many races, the picking of a horse to finish second should be easier than picking a winner, if only through a process of gradual elimination. It must be remembered, too, that the term "second" implies "or better," meaning that the selector is free from the mental hazard of having to peg it exactly, or else.

However, where this betting system is concerned, it is best to go along with a selector who, when he picks a horse to finish second, means that the horse will finish second. Because the whole plan is to bet the second choice to place, and nothing else, the less that the rest of the betting public goes along with that idea, the better for the bettor.

That brings up the betting public. It swings to two extremes. The "risk" school favors a straight bet. The "safe" players go for show. The "in-betweeners," or place bettors, fill out the picture as a sort of compromise. But when it comes to promoting a second choice to a winner, the pendulum is apt to swing wider. The lure is to make a straight bet and cash in heavier than usual. The common-sense attitude is to buy a show ticket and get that extra insurance.

MIDDLE ODDS AND OVERLAYS

This system says: Do neither. Take the selector's second choice and bet it to come in second, exactly as he figured it should. In that way, you aim to hit the betting peak, whether in terms of frequency, or price, or both. The purpose is to avoid any speculation on straight bets and to ignore the security promised by show bets, because both should be the slopes of the hump represented by the place bets, which are the only play in this system.

To put this to the test, the table on the following pages gives the results of four different selections covering the same series of forty-five races. Where the same figures occur, they signify identical choices. All represent horses picked to finish *second* in the race, not first. For convenience, the Selectors will be listed as A, B, C, and D. Others could have been included, but these represented well-established Selectors in relation to this particular track. It will be quite apparent, however, that there is considerable variance in their choice of seconds.

Note that with A, B, and C, the place earnings all represented a peak as compared with straight and show. Though A did scarcely better than break even, B brought in a healthy profit of $24.70 (more than 25 percent of the $90 wagered), while C, which represented the consensus, registered a 10 percent gain. With D, the preponderance of show in the last two days wiped out the early gain on place and resulted in a sizable loss. In short, the horses that D picked to run second mostly came in third.

Much depends on the player picking the selector rather than the horses. Selections and results must first be studied to find a consistent selector where choices to finish second are concerned. From then on, such selections are bet to place only, as already stated.

Normally, the Track Man's selections should show consistency in picking horses to place, so they should always be checked, if only for comparison with others. A consensus may prove less reliable, as its second choices are a composite of first, seconds and thirds.

SELECTIVE PLACE SYSTEM

DAY	RACE	A STRAIGHT	A PLACE	A SHOW	B STRAIGHT	B PLACE	B SHOW	C STRAIGHT	C PLACE	C SHOW	D STRAIGHT	D PLACE	D SHOW
FIRST DAY	1		4.30	3.20		4.30	3.20						
	2	8.30	4.80	3.80					8.20	5.60		8.20	5.60
	3								4.50	3.30			
	4				5.70		2.40			3.80	5.70	3.50	2.40
	5		4.30	2.70		3.50	8.50			2.40		4.30	3.50
	6					4.10	3.50		4.10	3.50		4.10	3.50
	7					5.40	3.50						
	8		4.60	4.00		4.60	4.00		4.60	4.00			
	9												
	Total	**8.30**	**18.00**	**13.70**	**5.70**	**21.90**	**25.10**		**21.40**	**22.60**	**5.70**	**20.10**	**15.00**
SECOND DAY	1	5.40	3.20	2.70	5.40	7.60	4.50				5.40	7.60	4.50
	2	8.00	3.50	3.00		3.20	2.70		3.50			3.20	2.70
	3		4.30	3.90	5.00	3.30	3.00		4.30	3.00			
	4			3.20	23.20	6.30	2.80	8.00		3.90			
	5						3.90			3.20			
	6					6.20	3.90			2.30			
	7						5.40				5.10		2.90
	8		2.60	2.30					2.60			3.40	
	9												
	Total	**13.40**	**13.60**	**15.10**	**33.60**	**26.60**	**26.20**	**8.00**	**10.40**	**12.40**	**10.50**	**14.20**	**10.10**
THIRD DAY	1		4.10	2.70					3.70	3.10	10.20	5.20	3.80
	2			2.90			3.60	7.90	6.30	3.60		5.30	3.60
	3		3.50	3.10		6.30	4.10		6.70	4.10		6.30	4.00
	4			3.10	13.50	6.70	3.10	13.50		3.20		3.50	3.10
	5						3.10			2.90			3.20
	6		4.10	3.40		3.50	3.50					3.70	2.90
	7						3.50	6.40	3.70		6.40	3.40	3.50
	8								3.40				
	9												
	Total		**11.70**	**15.20**	**13.50**	**16.50**	**20.90**	**27.80**	**23.80**	**16.90**	**16.60**	**27.40**	**24.10**

SELECTIVE PLACE SYSTEM

	A			B			C			D		
RACE	STRAIGHT	PLACE	SHOW	STRAIGHT	PLACE	SHOW	STRAIGHT	PLACE	SHOW	STRAIGHT	PLACE	SHOW
FOURTH DAY												
1	5.00			5.20	3.20	3.00	5.20	3.20	3.00			
2		2.60	2.40		3.80	3.30		3.80	3.30			
3												4.10
4												3.10
5												
6	15.00	11.00	5.80		11.00	5.80		11.00	5.80			2.70
7	9.90	5.20	3.00						2.70			3.00
8	10.10	4.10	3.00		3.50	2.60			3.00			3.90
9		5.10	3.60			3.90						
	40.00	**28.00**	**17.80**	**5.20**	**21.50**	**18.60**	**5.20**	**18.00**	**17.80**			**16.80**
FIFTH DAY												
1	6.30	3.60	3.00									3.50
2		3.80	2.90		3.80	2.90		3.80	2.90			3.10
3			3.00	10.10	4.50	3.40					3.60	
4	5.10	3.60	2.80		5.90	3.60	5.10	3.60	2.80			4.10
5		2.50	2.30				9.10	2.90	2.50			
6					7.60	4.30			3.20			3.20
7		3.30	2.50		3.30	2.50		3.30	2.50			
8						2.60		8.50	3.90			
9		3.70	2.80	6.50	3.10	2.50		3.70	2.80	32.80	3.70	2.80
	11.40	**20.50**	**19.30**	**16.60**	**28.20**	**21.80**	**14.20**	**25.80**	**20.60**	**32.80**	**7.30**	**16.70**
TOTALS	73.10	91.80	81.10	74.60	114.70	112.60	55.20	99.40	90.30	90.00	69.00	82.70
INVESTMENT	90.00	90.00	90.00	90.00	90.00	90.00	90.00	90.00	90.00	90.00	90.00	90.00

3. THE SELECTIVE MIDDLE-ODDS SYSTEM

Here is a betting method based on a selector's ratings of the in-between horses that are above the favorite class of 2 to 1 and below the long-shot rating of 6 to 1 or higher. Since the mid-point is 4 to 1, that is taken as the basis.

Take these steps in making your selections:

Study the ratings of a recognized selector who lists every horse in the race according to its probable odds, and check off any horses that are rated at 4 to 1. These are the horses to play, provided that the odds on the next horse do not jump to 10 to 1 or higher.

Unless there are some horses rated between 4 to 1 and 10 to 1, pass up the race, as there may be too much betting on the 4 to 1 selection.

If there is no horse rated at 4 to 1, a 5 to 1 horse is acceptable on the same basis—but not a 3 to 1 selection, as you are hoping for long odds, so you cannot begin too low.

If there are two or more horses rated at 4 to 1, all must be considered. In that case, watch the tote board—and play the one with the highest odds as post time approaches. The idea is to cash in on a long shot whenever possible.

The theory behind the system is that the selector must regard the horse as having real potential, or he would not rate it as low as 4 to 1. If the odds drop before the race, the horse may loom as a favorite, yet not at too low a price. If they climb high, you still have a reasonably sound bet according to expert opinion, and that gives you a really playable long shot.

Now let's see how the system works in practice according to some actual charts.

MIDDLE ODDS AND OVERLAYS

RACE	WIN	PLACE	SHOW	RACE	WIN	PLACE	SHOW
MIDDLE ODDS SYSTEM IN PRACTICE							
1	....	....	....	34	....	3.40	2.30
2	$11.70	$6.20	$4.50	35	....	....	....
3		....	....	36	....	....	....
4	14.70	5.70	4.30	37*	....	5.30	2.70
5	....	....	....	38	....	6.30	5.10
6	....	3.70	2.90	39	....	3.50	2.40
7*	....	....	4.10	40	9.40	4.80	3.70
8*	....	....	....	41	....	....	....
9	....	....	3.50	42	....	....	....
10	....	....	....	43	....	....	....
11	6.00	4.10	2.70	44	....	....	$6.00
12	6.80	3.50	3.10	45	....	....	3.00
13	....	....	....	46	....	....	....
14	....	....	....	47	....	....	....
15	....	5.00	2.90	48	....	....	2.30
16	....	....	....	49	....	....	2.90
17	5.70	3.50	2.40	50	...	...	...
18	....	....	....	51	....	$2.40	2.10
19	....	....	....	52	....	....	4.50
20	....	....	3.70	53	$33.80	13.90	4.80
21	....	....	3.40	54	....	11.60	6.30
22*	...	...	...	55	....	9.80	4.20
23	....	$5.30	$3.80	56	....	....	4.40
24*	....	...	3.50	57	8.00	3.80	3.10
25	$61.50	17.20	7.00	58	....	....	....
26	....	....	....	59	4.00	3.20	2.70
27	....	....	....	60	....	....	....
28	10.10	5.10	3.60	61	12.80	4.80	3.00
29	....	....	....	62*	....	....	2.70
30	....	3.70	2.80	63	....	....	...
31	8.30	4.10	2.90	**Total**	**$201.90**	**$144.00**	**$132.40**
32	9.10	4.10	3.10	**Bet**	**126.00**	**126.00**	**126.00**
33	....	....	....	**Profit**	**$75.90**	**$18.55**	**$6.40**

This system is designed for straight play in order to cash in heavily on the long shots that it occasionally produces. Figures are given on place and show to illustrate how they fell below the straight bet returns in this series. The extra margin on the straight total came chiefly from the long-shot wins in Races 25 and 53.

These were not the only long shots in the series. In the first race, a horse with a 4 to 1 rating zoomed to 20 to 1 at post time, but failed to show. The fifth race offered a truly phenomenal chance at 40 to 1, which also proved a dud. A 12 to 1 shot missed in the eighteenth race, and a 20 to 1 fell through in the sixtieth race. The horse that paid $6 on show (in the forty-fourth race) was running at 13 to 1.

Ordinarily, none of those horses would be worth backing if a player simply went by the final figures that he saw flashing on the tote board, but starting from a selector's rating of 4 to 1, they just can't be as bad as the figures would indicate. Remember, though, that the presence of other horses rating between 4 to 1 and 10 to 1 has much to do with it, as heavy betting on such nags will often cause one to be neglected. That's the one to pick, if he was good enough to rate a 4 to 1 beforehand.

Note that, in referring to the chart, the races marked with an asterisk indicate that the odds went up on two horses that were rated at 4 to 1, and that there was still a close choice at post time. If the player had chosen the "other" horse, the tally would have run:

RACE	WIN	PLACE	SHOW
7	12.70	5.20	3.00
8	....	8.10	4.00
22	....	4.40	3.30
24	7.90	3.70	3.10
37	10.60	5.20	2.90
62	....	3.70	2.80

If such horses had been played, they would have increased the straight bet profits by 40 per cent, while the place returns would have more than doubled and show would have just about doubled, as follows:

	STRAIGHT	PLACE	SHOW
Original Profit	75.90	18.00	6.40
Added Profit	31.20	25.00	6.10
Potential Total	$107.10	$43.00	$12.50

These higher returns are somewhat speculative, but chances are that the player would have cashed in on a goodly portion of them, particularly on place and show wagers. Like many systems, this one may vary according to the selector and the track, so the combination should be given a preliminary test for its consistency before risking a play.

Such a test may also determine the type of play. As an example, a test of fifteen races at an Eastern track brought no wins at all on straight bets, while the returns were $31.50 on place and only $23.30 on show.

On a $30 play, place alone showed a meager $1.50 profit, so a player should logically have proceeded with place wagers only, or else ignored the system as too doubtful under these circumstances.

4. THE MOVING-UP METHOD

This is a neat switch from a commonly accepted form of play. Everyone knows that when a horse finishes in the money for a few races in a row, it is likely to be nearing its peak form. The trouble is that too many people know it and the odds drop on that horse, so that when playing it brings a win, it comes through at too low a price.

The moving-up method covers that. Its idea is to catch the winner *before* the general public moves in on the deal. This is done by watching horses that fail to finish in the money, and then grabbing on to them immediately after they show the proper symptoms. In short, symptom is converted into system.

Whether you watch the losers until they take off, or simply check back on horses that finish in the money, it all amounts to the same thing. The horse you want is the one that has lost twice in a row and then finishes first, second or third. The worse it lost before that, the better. But once it has climbed into the money, it's your baby.

The one and only rule is to bet that horse in its next race. If it wins, that's it. If it fails to finish in the money, back it again in its next race. Here is the theory behind the system: The fact that after failing twice, the horse showed ability on its third try, is an indication that it is coming up. Perhaps it is; perhaps it isn't. That is the risk involved in the system. But the risk itself may pay dividends. When the player catches a winner, he is ahead of the other bettors. That more than makes up for the losses, according to the proponents of this system.

Now comes the question: Should each horse be played for straight, place or show?

Some reliable statistics indicate that straight bets are best. The reason is fairly evident. The horse is a potential winner, so the sooner it is bet as such, the bigger the odds should be. If other players like the horse, they may nibble first with show, then with place. So the odds may not be proportionately high in those departments. At the same time, they may be high enough to pay off in their own right, thus serving an insurance purpose. This depends on the extent of the player's bankroll. If it can stand the strain, straight bets are the play, because this system is apt to bring in some surprising long shots. A horse that has gone from bad to worse is not apt to rouse public confidence by a better showing in a single race. People may begin to back it, but hardly on an all-out basis. They want to see it show again, but the system player doesn't wait—not if he's playing this system. He just moves in ahead and cashes in on the surprise.

The same applies to the "repeat" if the horse fails to finish in the money the first time it is bet. Then the general public will really be off it, figuring that its one brief showing was a dud. But the horse may still be improving and again the system player is banking on that possibility.

Again, the straight play may prove the most productive, as the horse is likely to come through as a winner if it does anything at all. But bets to place or show may serve a useful purpose, so there is no good reason to reject them. All this can be clarified by a reference to the following list, wherein the horses were taken in strictly alphabetical order regardless of track and exact date.

The one thing that all these horses hold in common is that each was an also ran in its first race and in its second race, but that it finished in the money on its third try. The results listed below were those of each horse's fourth race, the only race on which a wager was made, unless the horse failed to show. In that case, the horse's fifth race is listed as a repeat.

FOURTH RACE RESULTS

HORSE	STR.	PLACE	SHOW
Abbe's Time	...	$4.80	$3.20
Ace Trophy	...	...	3.50
Acquiescence	...	3.50	2.50
Add-A-Bet	...	3.20	2.40
Adelantado	...	...	...
(Repeat)	...	...	...
Adlibit	$13.40	7.00	5.20
Admired	...	...	...
(Repeat)	...	...	...
Adorable Sis	7.60	3.60	2.80
Aggie Forever	...	...	3.10
Aggie's Boy	...	...	...
(Repeat)	...	...	10.00
Air Commander	...	6.30	3.60
Air Defense	69.80	12.00	6.60
Air Express	...	...	...
(Repeat)	15.80	9.30	7.20
Alexis	10.10	4.10	3.20
Alfa	7.20	4.30	3.60
Alfild	26.50	9.50	12.50
Alfine	...	4.70	2.80
Alflos	...	...	...
(Repeat)	...	...	...
Alford Stuart	...	...	...
(Repeat)	$7.20	$3.60	No Show

FOURTH RACE RESULTS

HORSE	STR.	PLACE	SHOW
Ali Bye Bye	...	3.40	$2.40
Alibi Betty	...	...	5.00
Alice Brujo	...	2.60	2.60
All at Once	10.10	3.70	2.90
Alport	6.10	3.60	2.80
Altar Boy	8.50	3.50	3.10
Alwhirl	...	...	...
(Repeat)	...	7.90	5.50
Amarillo Kid	...	...	4.10
American Flyer	...	...	...
(Repeat)	10.30	4.60	3.80
American Wolf	2.80	3.00	2.90
Anacar	...	...	...
(Repeat)	...	...	...
Anayr	...	...	...
(Repeat)	...	...	...
Andrea Kay	...	...	...
(Repeat)	...	8.90	7.00
Angle Bar	33.80	6.60	5.50
Ann's Sultan	...	2.90	3.00
TOTALS	$229.20	$126.60	$123.80
Bet	$90.00	$90.00	$88.00
Profit	$139.20	$36.60	$34.80

5. THE THIRD-BEST HORSE

The theory behind this mode of play is simple. At many tracks, the favorites show a good percentage of wins if backed regularly; but they are played too heavily to show a profit. In contrast, the second favorite, or contender, as the next best tote board choice is termed, may offer much better odds, but fall short on the required number of wins.

Sometimes the two horses with the lowest tote board odds are too close to allow a choice between them. There is always the chance that either or both may be a false favorite, whose odds have dropped while "smart money" bettors have been holding back long enough for the public to go all out on the wrong horse or horses. In that case, the more the profit that is likely to accrue to some other capable but neglected steed. Next in line is the third-best horse, because:

a. It must be worth a bet, or so many players would not be backing it ahead of the rest.

b. If the smart money is not on the first two choices, the third is the next where it should be expected.

How well this works out is best illustrated by the following charts, which cover the third-best selections at a Southern track over a twelve-day period. These are based on a $2 wager: straight, place and show, as listed in the chart. These results, though not spectacular, reveal a slow but worthwhile profit on a straight play. The score was practically even after the sixth race, so that a small investment would have turned the trick.

However, the long adverse runs (races 39-60 inclusive) could have proven devastating earlier. Thus, place bets would have been safer, as is also demonstrated in the results of the ninth day (races 65-72 inclusive), where wagers on place produced a very tidy profit.

Betting to show resulted in only a slight loss, but chances of profit are not good in that department, as too many conservative bettors are apt to ride along on a show basis, bringing the odds too far down.

In short, the player who backs the third-best horse to win is apt to catch some nice overlays that will prove real profit-makers. A few such might come through with place bets. However, show should not ordinarily be considered, though it offers money-making opportunities on a progressive play, as will be detailed later.

Here, however, we are considering only flat or uniform bets, which can, of course, be wagered in multiples of $2. A $10 flat bet, for example, would have brought a profit of $151 over the twelve-day period, if played on a straight basis.

MIDDLE ODDS AND OVERLAYS

RESULTS OF BETTING THE THIRD-BEST HORSE			
RACE	STR.	PLACE	SHOW
1	...	...	...
2	...	...	...
3	...	...	...
4	...	...	...
5	...	...	...
6	$11.40	$6.20	$4.60
7	9.80	5.20	4.00
8	...	...	...
9	...	...	...
10		6.80	5.40
11	9.40	4.60	3.60
12	...	...	...
13	...	...	...
14		9.00	5.80
15	...	...	...
16		3.80	3.80
17	...	...	5.80
18	...	5.80	4.00
19	10.80	5.80	4.80
20	...	3.90	2.60
21	...	...	...
22	9.40	3.60	2.80
23	...	...	...
24	...	...	...
25	...	...	...
26	12.40	5.20	4.20
27	...	...	...
28	10.40	7.00	4.60
29	...	...	...
30	...	...	...
31	18.40	6.00	3.80
32	...	...	...
33	...	$7.20	$4.20
34	...	...	...
35	...	4.00	2.80
36	...	...	...
37	$10.40	5.20	4.80
38	10.60	5.20	3.00
39	...	...	...
40	...	...	...
41	...	...	...
42	...	5.20	4.40
43	...	4.60	3.20
44	...	...	5.00
45	...	...	...
46	...	...	...
47	...	...	...
48	...	...	...
49	...	6.60	5.40
50	...	...	4.50

RESULTS OF BETTING THE THIRD-BEST HORSE			
RACE	STR.	PLACE	SHOW
51	7.80	5.00	3.40
52	...	...	...
53	...	...	3.80
54	...	...	...
55	...	...	...
56	...	...	...
57	...	...	...
58	...	5.60	4.60
59	...	...	...
60	...	...	...
61	20.60	15.20	3.20
62	...	...	2.80
63	...	...	...
64	15.40	6.60	6.20
65	...	...	...
66	...	$4.60	$3.80
67	...	5.20	4.40
68	...	...	...
69	...	...	...
70	...	5.20	3.20
71	...	9.40	5.40
72	...	...	4.40
73	$13.60	7.80	4.40
74	...	...	...
75	...	...	...
76	9.80	5.20	2.80
77	...	5.80	3.60
78	...	...	3.20
79	...	...	...
80	9.80	5.60	5.80
81	...	...	...
82	...	...	...
83	...	...	...
84	...	...	4 .00
85	...	...	...
86	8.60	4.20	2 .40
87	...	...	...
88	...	...	...
89	...	...	...
90	...	...	...
91	3.60	2.80	2.40
92	...	...	...
93	12.60	5.00	3.20
94	...	...	...
95	11.40	4.60	3.60
96	...	...	...
Total:	$226.20	$208.60	$177.10
Bets	196.00	196.00	196.00
Profit /Loss	$30.20	$12.60	(-$14.90)

How dependable these third-best bets may prove is a question in its own right. The charts listed here were from a Southern track where the betting was strong enough to bring down the odds on the first two horses without overly affecting the third-best steed. This is the ideal setup for such play.

In contrast, here are returns from a Northern track where the daily betting was on a bigger basis. The results are given by day's totals instead of race by race:

RESULTS FROM NORTHERN TRACK			
DAY	**STRAIGHT**	**PLACE**	**SHOW**
1st Day	....	$9.50	$13.40
2nd Day	$46.70	23.20	14.90
3rd Day	11.80	5.40	8.70
4th Day	16.00	12.00	14.50
5th Day	11.00	11.50	8.40
6th Day	11.90	21.50	16.30
7th Day	$33.30	$17.10	$19.50
8th Day	20.10	10.20	7.90
9th Day	10.50	13.20	13.80
10th Day	12.90	5.80	7.70
11th Day	....	....	7.90
12th Day	7.30	14.90	9.70
Bets	**$192.00**	**$192.00**	**$192.00**
Returns	181.50	144.30	142.70
Loss	**$10.50**	**$47.70**	**$49.30**

This would indicate that the increased number of bettors either brought down the third-horse odds too much, or caused confusion as to which horse actually was the third best. This conclusion is borne out by statistics from a still larger track, where the falloff was too marked to allow any play of the third-horse method.

6. THE FOURTH-BEST HORSE

This is an extension of the third-best play. It goes on the assumption that if the first and second favorites are being bet down, the same may apply to the third favorite, too. In that case the fourth-best horse should be the one that promises the "mostest for the leastest." If the odds on the fourth-best horse begin to dwindle, chances are that smart money is riding with it. If the odds hang high, the horse may be an overlay and is worth a bet on that count. That, at least, is the thinking behind such betting procedure.

The advantage to the casual player is that the fourth-best horse is often well defined and more easily identified than those with lower odds. While the odds may fluctuate, they are sometimes high enough for a single race to bring in a profit on a day's play. Since this puts the fourth best into a long-shot category, straight bets are the logical type for such play.

The general purpose is to cash in as much as possible when one of these horses does win, thus depending upon return rather than frequency as the money-making factor.

The accompanying charts give the results of straight bets on the fourth-best horse over twelve consecutive days at five different major tracks. All were taken from the closing odds and only the winning races are listed.

	TRACK A	TRACK B	TRACK C	TRACK D	TRACK E
RESULTS OF STRAIGHT BETS ON THE FOURTH-BEST HORSE					
DAY	WINS	WINS	WINS	WINS	WINS
1st	13.10 10.50	13.80 22.40 15.00	19.20	...	13.00
2nd	12.90	17.20	15.20 17.40	14.40	...
3rd	14.00	13.40	11.20	16.70	9.10 13.30
4th	...	11.80	...	10.80	...
5th	12.30 22.40	...	...	14.70 20.80	11.00
6th	17.40 14.10	...	19.00	10.70	19.70 13.10 14.80
7th	14.40	12.80 16.20 33.60	19.20 10.40	10.50	12.50
8th	13.30	11.40	...	...	...
9th	20.50	12.40	15.40	15.60 20.90	19.70 12.30
10th	...	12.80	13.20	11.20	11.60 21.80
11th	20.40	8.60	17.20 10.80	12.10 25.70	12.50 17.70
12th	16.90 10.10	...	12.60	13.80	17.50
Return	$212.30	201.40	180.80	197.90	219.60
Bet	192.00	192.00	192.00	192.00	192.00
Won	$20.30	$9.40	$11.20	$5.90	$27.60

8 THE WEIGHT FACTOR

There are various ways of equalizing the chances of horses in a race so as to make it a close contest. These have been reduced to one common denominator: weight. The assumption is that the more weight a horse carries, the slower it will run. But when the difference is only a few pounds, much can be argued pro and con regarding the weight factor. Of prime importance is the fact that as a horse gains in age, strength and maturity, it should be able to carry more weight than formerly. Hence every track in the United States goes by an official scale of weights that automatically assigns added poundage to older horses unless otherwise specified.

The corollary to that proposition is that added distance increases the burden of such weight, so reductions are made in longer races, with horses of various ages. This is also covered in the same official scale. In some races, fillies and mares are given a few pounds' deduction because they belong to the "weaker sex." Some players regard that as a good reason never to back them. Now, this is good as far as it goes, but it cannot cover every individual case, far from it. Some horses, like humans, are slower to reach maturity than others. Some have a way of taking everything in stride, including weight.

But disregarding those points, we have the question: Just how much should added poundage retard the average horse's speed?

Generally figured, the answer is that 4 to 5 pounds are the equivalent of about one-fifth of a second, which is the time a horse supposedly takes to travel a single length. Though this is something like taking the price per pound of meat, potatoes and coffee and multiplying them to learn the cost of a steak dinner, it works out pretty well.

Call it 5 pounds for a short sprint, 4 pounds for races up to a mile and 3 pounds in anything over that distance, all in terms of a single length, as the horse will be losing speed at the end of a long run. Besides, lengths and fractions thereof are the measuring stick by which a player wins or loses.

If all weights were assigned according to the official scale, it would be easy to tell how obligingly the horses themselves conformed to those set rules. But most races go by conditions of their own, which vary the weights accordingly.

THREE TYPES OF WEIGHT-ADJUSTED RACES

The three types of weight-adjusted races are allowance races, claiming races, and handicap races.

1. ALLOWANCE RACES

In allowance races, horses are given basic weights, and are then "allowed" specific reductions according to their recent showings, or rather to their lack of recent good showings. In short, poor past performance is a factor in a horse's favor.

2. CLAIMING RACES

In claiming races, similar allowances are commonly granted, but here the claiming price may influence the weight factor, since horses are sometimes granted a weight reduction if offered at amounts below the top claiming price.

3. HANDICAP RACES

In handicap races, the track handicapper assigns weights which in his judgment should equalize the horses. Such races often result in remarkably close finishes, including a surprising percentage of dead heats, which makes the weight factor seem all-important. But such races attract steeds of a high caliber that are in the proper fettle for an all-out effort.

Some students of the turf have pointed out that horses may finish far behind in handicap races, greatly outclassed despite the supposed equality of the weight factor, proving that the urge to win is not always enough to keep a nag in the running, even when it is well ridden.

THE ROLE OF THE JOCKEY

This brings up another phase of the weight factor: the jockey. Apprentice jockeys are allowed a weight reduction, usually of five pounds, because of their inexperience as riders. So in theory at least, a skilled jockey should be able to boot a horse home a length or more ahead of a less able rider. That being generally conceded, how can it be expressed in terms of fixed weight, when the jockeys themselves may vary not only in shades of degrees, but in their knowledge of special racing skills?

Some players answer that question by betting on the jockeys rather than the horses. That in turn brings another frequently discussed phase of the weight factor, the difference between "live" and "dead" weight.

Live weight represents that of the jockey's own weight, whereas dead weight consists of lead slugs that are added to the horse's saddle in order to make up the required total. Thus if two horses should be slated to carry 115 pounds, one ridden by a jockey weighing 115 pounds would be carrying all "live" weight; while if the other had a 104-pound rider, it would require 11 additional pounds of "dead" weight.

And this, some authorities claim, can mean the difference between a "live" and a "dead" horse, so far as winning chances are concerned. They cite the fact that modem jockeys do not sit erect upon their chargers as did armored knights in days of yore. Instead, they lay forward on the horse's shoulders, adapting themselves to the steed's stride. This obviously eases the horse's burden, whereas the lead weights are still like so much armor.

The weight factor itself dates back to a period before the development of the present riding technique, so the "live" and "dead" notion has definite merit. Some students of the subject regard one pound of dead weight as equal to two pounds of live weight. Thus in the example just cited, the horse with the 115-pound jockey would be carrying its proper quota, but the steed with the 104-pound rider would be burdened with the equivalent of 126 pounds and therefore wouldn't stand a chance.

Other theorists have supported the two-pounds-for-one idea with the argument that a skilled jockey, geared to the horse's gait, is practically in the air half the time, so his weight is only half the burden. By that token, if the jockey wore a money belt containing three pounds in silver dollars, it would become live weight instead of dead. Every now and then a skittish horse throws its jockey at the start of a race, yet stays right along with the pack. But it doesn't outdistance the rest by twenty to twenty-five lengths, as it very well might, on the basis of five pounds representing one length. The determining factor in this case is the jockey, not the weight, or lack of it.

So many things can account for a horse losing or gaining a length or two somewhere in the race that the weight factor, even if measurable to the last ounce, may be counteracted or nullified. The fact that a horse itself weighs in the neighborhood of a thousand pounds has also been advanced as a reason why a difference of only a few pounds-give or take-should not matter too much in the outcome of a race.

Some analysts have argued that if two men of equal weight entered a 100-yard dash, one in a tracksuit, the other in regular clothes, the burden of added weight would be very obvious. But it doesn't apply with horses, as they habitually carry a hundred pounds or more.

Start two men in a running race, each carrying a fifteen-pound pack on his back, and it is very unlikely that one would gain a great advantage if allowed to discard a shaving kit from his pack. But proportionately that is about the difference in dead weight as carried by two closely rated horses.

Many experts agree that weight is a bigger factor on a muddy track than when the track is dry and fast. The extra poundage slows the horses more than usual, so the advantage may be with those that are carrying less weight. But some steeds are good "mudders" regardless. That has to be taken into consideration, too.

Owners and trainers may put a veteran jockey on a horse, even though it means adding a few pounds over the weight allotted for that race. They apparently feel that the horse has shown an ability to carry up to a certain limit, so that the extra poundage will not matter if the horse will give a better effort with the right jockey. In contrast, a horse that dislikes weight may do its best with an apprentice prentice jockey in the saddle, thanks to the lessened poundage granted.

Thus the rule that weight is the great equalizer may apply to some horses but not to all. This can be further expressed by the fact that a good horse may still do well despite additional weight, but a poor horse can't be turned into a good one simply by taking weight off it. That's one reason why many players give little or no heed to weight, but look for other angles. They may decide that weights actually do equalize or that they don't matter at all; in either case, something else beside weight must account for one horse coming in ahead of another.

On the contrary, the weight factor may itself be used as a means of system play. Some of the methods appear in the following pages.

WEIGHT SYSTEM #1: WEIGHT RATING SYSTEM

This way of picking horses is based on the theory that the greater the amount of weight assigned to a horse, the better its rating should be, which gives it the best chance of coming home a winner. Working from that basis, all fixed-weight races are eliminated, along with maidens and two-year-olds. In all the remaining events, weights are noted and play is made on the horse carrying the most weight.

If two horses are carrying the same weight, the best rule is to watch the tote board and back the one showing the lowest odds shortly before post time.

If three or more horses are carrying the same weight, the simplest rule is to pass up the race. This also applies to any races that appear too doubtful, as you are not compelled to bet every race.

In the broad form just given, you are aiming for the following advantages:

1. With the horse a favorite, its chances should be unusually good. Whether or not the top weight will retard the steed's running is a question; but there is no doubt that it retards a group of bettors who shy away from over-weights. As a result, you rarely pick a false favorite by this method.

2. Overweight spells overlays, for the same reason. The more money that goes on the other horses,

the better the odds where the top-weight horse is concerned.

3. Long shots are especially attractive with this system, because in theory at least, the horse with the most weight definitely belongs in the race, which isn't true of all long shots. Again, most long-shot players go after low-weight horses. So the play of a neglected "heavy" offers a double advantage.

RESULTS FOR 30 RACES

Over a series of thirty races at a popular Southern track, this system delivered the following results:

Straight: A play of $60 brought $93.10 (5 winners)
Place: A play of $60 brought $76.43 (13 seconds)
Show: A play of $60 brought $73.70 (18 thirds)
Across the Board: A play of $180 brought $243.23

Note that the preponderance of the return was on the straight bets and the lowest take on show. This is as it should be, because the theory is that you are backing the best horse in each race, though you need the place and show money in case one or two prove to be better.

RESULTS FOR 30 MORE RACES

The same pattern appeared in a second series of thirty races at the same track, where the results were closer to the cushion, but still showed profits in all departments:

Straight: A play of $60 brought $71.10 (9 winners)
Place: A play of $60 brought $67.40 (13 seconds)
Show: A play of $60 brought $62.00 (15 thirds)
Across the Board: A play of $180 brought $200.50

These figures, while too small to be conclusive, at least indicate the pattern of the play. Note that the series with the fewest winners brought the greatest cash return. That fits with the theory on which the system is based—namely, that extra weight may worry the betting public more than the horse that carries it.

Still, to depend on winners alone would be skating on thin ice, even in a tropical clime. Place and show wagers not only are good insurance; as a rule, they bring better than average prices with this system.

From comparative studies, this betting method works better at the bigger tracks, where class is a bigger factor. At tracks where the attendance and the daily handle are small, a player is apt to encounter a steady loss. It is wise to check results at individual tracks to see if the system is playable, either in its simple form (as described) or with certain modifications.

MODIFICATIONS OF WEIGHT SYSTEM #1

Rather than complicate the system with too many arbitrary rules, it should be limited along definite lines, such as:

When two horses are carrying the highest weight, bet both across the board. This allows for a high-odds win, which is the main aim of the system. Since both horses can finish in the money, such a play is worth the added costs. Also, there will be no regrets if the horse with shorter odds proves to be the wrong one.

Pass up races where more than two horses are grouped within two pounds of the highest weight, particularly if the field is large. Since the idea is to profit by the shyness of the betting public toward "overweight" horses, that factor must be strongly apparent. In short, tighten the choice when it looks doubtful.

Limit the bets to handicap races in which the track handicapper assigns the weights in an attempt to equalize the finish. Naturally, he has to put the most weight on the horse that he thinks is the best and he can't overdo it or his judgment will be questioned later. Actually, he is picking your play for you. So the policy is to go along with it.

WEIGHT SYSTEM #2: AVERAGE WEIGHT SYSTEM

Here is perhaps the simplest of all weight rating systems, and its results on certain tracks mark it as one of the best, at least where those courses are concerned. As with many systems, it can be tightened for play at other tracks, but it is given first in its basic form. Consider only races with a wide variance of weights, eliminating maidens, two-year-olds or any others that you may consider doubtful. Then apply the following rule:

Add the weights of all the horses in the race and divide the total by the number of horses, to strike an average weight. Consider all the horses carrying more than that weight and pick the one with the lowest odds at post time.

For example, there are nine horses in the race, with weights and odds as follows:

AVERAGE WEIGHT SYSTEM		
HORSE	**WEIGHT**	**ODDS**
A	116	8 to 1
B	111	2 to 1
C	10	32 to 1
D	116	5 to 1
E	115	9 to 1
F	113	8 to 1
G	107	4 to 1
H	105	70 to 1
I	112	7 to 1
Average	**111.5**	

Added, the weights come to 1,005. Divided by 9 (the number of horses), we find the average weight to be about 111½, so that the only horses to be considered are those carrying 112 pounds or over.

Of these, five horses qualify: A, D, E, F, and I. The horse with the lowest odds in that group was D. This horse won the race, paying $12.90 straight, $5.90 to place and $4.50 to show. The next two horses were B and C; neither was considered because they carried below-average weight.

RESULTS FOR 30 RACES

Over a series of thirty races, the results were:

Straight: A play of $60 brought $85.70 (10 winners)
Place: A play of $60 brought $92.90 (20 seconds)
Show: A play of $60 brought $77.60 (23 thirds)
Across the Board: $180 brought $256.20

The theory of this system is as simple as the play itself. On the assumption that better horses are able to carry more weight, you look for winners in the top half only. While it means playing a fair percentage of favorites, there are frequent choices that may bring better odds. What's more, it eliminates some of the close choices that often cause worry. Quite often there will be just a few pounds difference between two steeds that are galloping around the track at practically the same odds. But if one is just above and the other is just below the average weight mark, you simply pick the one in the top bracket.

Often, however, there may be a close choice between two eligible horses, both in the upper group, but with odds practically identical as the tote board nears its final flickers. In that case, take the horse with the lower amount of weight, the one nearer to the average mark.

Here is an interesting example: In one race with the high average mark of 117, horse A was carrying 122 pounds at odds of 4 to 1, while horse B was carrying 120 pounds at odds of 5 to 1. Both were wavering between those two figures, so although A was the proper choice, a player might have grabbed B instead, rather than risk reaching the ticket window too late.

Horse A came in second, paying $6 to place and $5 to show, a nice return for this system. But the "unlucky" player who hastily picked horse B wouldn't have fared so badly either. Horse B, the close choice, proved to be the winner, paying $12.40 straight, $7.70 to place and $5.10 to show.

When two or more horses in the upper bracket are carrying the same weight, it is better to pass up the race if their odds appear to be about the same. The idea is to strike a balance between the two variables, weight and price, not just to rate horses that carry identical weight on the basis of price alone.

Elimination of doubtful races, including those where a majority of the horses are carrying the same weight, usually results in a tightening of the play. If it is "off" at a certain track, it is good policy to consider.

WEIGHT SYSTEM #3: THE AVERAGE HORSE METHOD

This modification of the average weight system is based on the assumption that the horse carrying closest to average weight is worth a play in its own right, rather than giving preference to those in the higher bracket. Add the weights carried by all the horses, divide by the number of horses and play the horse nearest to that figure. If you hit the average on the button, so much the better!

In the nine-horse race listed earlier, the average weight carried was about 111 ½ pounds. So horse B, which was carrying exactly 111 pounds, was the only choice. It came in second at 2 to 1, paying $4.10 to place and $3.40 to show. But odds are not

necessarily a factor in this method, which may mean playing anything from a favorite to a long shot, depending on which is the average horse.

If two horses are equal in weight, play the one with the lower odds, unless they are very close, in which case both may be played, rather than pass up a good price. However, you may limit your play where long shots are concerned, passing up any horse running at 15 to 1 or above.

If there is no horse playable at the exact weight, check up and down the scale, pound by pound, until you come to one. Again, in case two horses are carrying the same weight, give preference to the one with lower odds, but be wary where long shots are concerned.

This method makes it comparatively easy to pick a horse in advance and there is very little worry over the changes in the tote board. As long as the price stays within bounds, a player can stick with his horse, and any choice is usually limited to two horses. Frequently, wagers can be made soon after the windows open.

Comparisons show that this type of play brings results at tracks where the average weight system is apt to be off form. So it is advisable to test both over a series of races before deciding which to use.

RESULTS OF 24 RACES				
RACE	STRAIGHT	PLACE	SHOW	APPROX ODDS
1st	$12.30	$6.30	$3.80	5-1
2nd	...	7.00	4.00	7-1
3rd	.....	.....	.....	3-1
4th	.....	.....	.....	2-1
5th	.....	.....	.....	3-1
6th	14.20	7.80	5.00	6-1
7th	.....	.....	.....	9-2
8th	.....	3.40	3.10	5-2
9th	4.90	3.70	3.20	3-2
10th	.....	.....	.....	9-1
11th	.....	6.10	4.10	5-1
12th	16.00	6.80	4.90	7-1
13th	.....	.....	$3.40	3-1
14th	.....	.....	.....	7-1
15th	.....	$5.00	3.60	3-1
16th	.....	.....	.....	8-1
17th	.....	14.70	7.90	14-1
18th	$16.80	8.30	6.80	7-1
19th	.....	.....	.....	12-1
20th	16.70	6.30	3.00	7-1
21st	.....	.....	.....	7-1
22nd	.....	.....	.....	10-1
23rd	.....	.....	.....	5-2
24th	...	2.80	2.40	6-5
Totals:	$80.90	$78.20	$55.20	

Straight: $48 brings $80.90
Place: $48 brings $78.20
Show: $48 brings $55-20
Across the Board: $144 brings $214.30

WEIGHT SYSTEM #4: WEIGHT PLUS PRICE

This system represents an effort to balance the two factors of weight and price for the benefit of the steady player. In essence, it is simplicity itself.

1) After eliminating all races with fixed weights, as well as maiden races, two-year-olds and stake races, you check the weight assigned to each horse in a race that you intend to play.

2) Then you add the weight carried to the approximate odds on the horse. The lowest total is the basis for the bet.

It would be nice indeed to strike a low balance and immediately call it a play, but it doesn't work that easily, except in certain races where the contestants are few and the figures are well defined. Modifications must be introduced at the outset to make the races properly playable.

By the rating given, a horse with top weight of 122, running at 2 to 1, would be scored as 124, exactly the same as a horse with the low weight of 109 running at 15 to 1. The general idea is to avoid these extremes and catch a nice play that blends low weight with high odds.

A horse carrying 112 pounds and running at 5 to 1, with an index of 117, would be a more typical bet. The system itself takes care of that, usually producing a balanced horse with a reasonably low figure. The trouble is, it may produce several horses that add up to practically the same total in the same race.

Some of these must be eliminated along with other horses. Here is a set of rules that showed good results over a series of races at a major track.

RULES FOR USING WEIGHT SYSTEM #4

   a. If the horse with the lowest total (weight plus price) is the favorite, do not play it.

   b. Do not play any horse unless its odds are 3 to 1 and preferably higher, except when a race has only five or six horses.

   c. In case two or more horses add up to the same total, give preference to the horse with the lowest weight, provided its odds meet the requirement already stated.

   d. Playing two horses is allowable, if each has a total (weight plus price) well below all others. Coupled entries may be played if both show the lowest total.

   e. Individual judgment may be applied in close choices, but if there is too much doubt, pass up the race entirely.

RESULTS FOR 30 RACES

At the track mentioned, these rules, flexibly applied, brought highly attractive returns over a series of thirty races, as follows:

   Straight: A play of $60 brought $136.80 (10 winners)
   Place: A play of $60 brought $69.00 (13 seconds)
   Show: A play of $60 brought $67.00 (16 thirds)
   Across the Board: $180 brought $272.80

As an added attraction, there were six races in which a reasonable change in judgment would have produced three more wins totaling $17.90, five more places, netting $27.50, and six more shows for $22.80. This would have boosted the return to $341, representing a net profit of $161.

30 MORE RACE RESULTS

In a second series of thirty races at the same track, the results tallied as follows:

Straight: A play of $60 brought $87.80 (7 winners)
Place: A play of $60 brought $86.50 (12 seconds)
Show: A play of $60 brought $66.70 (13 thirds)
Across the Board: $180 brought $241.00

Here again, potential plays would have added $8.30 to the straight, $9 to the place and $8 to the show columns, raising the return to $266.30, representing a net profit of $86.30. For practical purposes, we can take the play as actually recorded, with 60 races bringing $224.60 straight, $155.50 to place, and $133.70 to show, totaling $518.80 across the board, for a profit of $158.80 over the $360 invested.

That, however, does not give a full picture of the play. At best, many of the choices will be guesswork when tabbed against the fluctuating odds of the tote board. Many close ones might have gone another way, while others could have caused a player to pass up a race.

A horse that is dropping rapidly in odds may suddenly become the right play and then eliminate itself by falling as low as 3 to 1 in betting odds. Generally speaking, the system allows for this: If a player misses a good bet in one race, luck may be with him in another.

Time must be allowed to reach the betting windows before they close, but this is no more difficult than in ordinary betting. Often, you can cross off horses with heavy weights and high odds, leaving only a few to watch on a "weight plus price" basis. By having the weight list handy, you can make a quick, simple addition in a matter of moments, the play being decided accordingly.

In the next chapter, we will get into a subject that is always hotly debated around the track—how to find long shots and how to make a profit at betting them.

9 PLAYING THE LONG SHOTS

Perhaps no other lament is more frequently expressed in horse racing circles than crying over the one that got away, the long shot that that paid 30 to 1, the horse you considered betting but passed in favor of the nag that came dead last. Some bettors dedicate themselves to finding the rare long shot that will lead them to the fabled pot of gold at the end of the rainbow.

This is not to say that betting long shots is never profitable, far from it. You can make some big scores picking the right horses in the right races. This chapter discusses several systems for finding and wagering on long shots in a more disciplined fashion that simply taking a shot in the dark.

LONG-SHOT SYSTEM #1: THE SIMPLE LONG-SHOT SYSTEM

This betting method is based on the proposition that any horse that finished in the money should be a possible winner in its next try. All a player has to do is check what each horse did on its last outing and consider those that belong in this category. From this list, he picks a long shot, which for practical purposes can be a horse with odds of 10 to 1 or higher. If none of the "money" horses show such odds, he passes up the race. It there are two or more such long shots in the race, he takes the one with the highest odds.

The fact that one horse may have won its last race while another finished second or third has no bearing on the choice. Each is considered equal unless the tote board, when nearing its closing moments, should flash identical odds, say 12 to 1, on both. In that case, take the horse that finished better in the previous race.

From a random run of thirty races, this system gave the following results:

HORSE	ODDS	STRAIGHT	PLACE	SHOW
A	19.10 to 1	$40.20	$10.40	$3.30
B	15 to 1	....	8.40	5.40
C	15.80 to 1	33.60	12.40	8.00
D	12.20 to 1	....	7.90	5.30
E	15.75 to 1	....	....	6.30
F	11.60 to 1	....	....	4.20
G	10.20 to 1	22.40	12.80	7.00
H	12.70 to 1	....	9.80	6.70
I	15.95 to 1	....	12.70	5.90
30 Races at $2 Total: $60		$96.20	$74.40	$52.10

These figures are in keeping with the common notion that long shots should be played on the nose rather than to place or show. The final category, in particular, is to be avoided. A straight play is preferred, though some long-shot enthusiasts like to make a place bet as well, hoping to lessen the gaps in the series with smaller but more frequent profits.

In the list given above, there were only 3 wins in 30 plays, or a 10 percent average. That is enough on a long-shot system calling for winning odds of 10 to 1 or higher, but too long a string of losers can run a player out of his own money. As indicated above, place bets may show twice the frequency of straight wins and are therefore helpful as a carry-over.

In listing eligible horses, it doesn't matter how long ago each ran its last race, or what type of a race it was. But in betting on a race, it is better to exclude maidens, which can't have had previous wins, and two-year-olds. Jumping races, however, are good for long-shot play.

LONG-SHOT SYSTEM #2: THE SELECTOR'S LONG SHOT SYSTEM

This is a way of using daily selections to pick winners with high odds, so that an average run of winners will produce a worthwhile profit. It is a compromise between playing the selected favorites, which win often, but yield too little return, and going after long shots, which are usually a total loss if picked at random, but have a reasonable chance of coming through when chosen more intelligently.

The basic plan is to go along with any selector whose choice is at strict variance with the others. Since this is against the average player's policy, it usually means that there is less wagering on such a horse, so that its odds stay high. In cases where the odds take a decided drop, it may be interpreted as advantageous, since the public itself is endorsing the offbeat selection.

This system can be used with any group of selectors whose picks appear in a daily newspaper or racing form. The only qualification is that there should be enough of these selectors to allow for potential long shots. The more thoroughly one selector's choice is ignored by all the rest, the better. In the examples that follow, seven selectors are considered, along with the consensus, consisting of their combined choices.

RULES FOR THE SELECTOR'S LONG-SHOT SYSTEM

In simplified form, the rules run as follows:

1. Check the consensus and eliminate all money horses; that is, those which are listed first, second or third. Since these are the top three of the combined selections, they are almost sure to be too heavily played.

2. Next, study the first choices of each individual selector. If any such horse has been picked by one selector only, it is the proper play. If there are two or more of these choices, all must be considered.

3. If no first choices qualify, look over the second choices of the individual selectors. Eliminate all of these that were named in the consensus or picked as first by an individual selector. If any that remain are picked as second choice by one selector only, consider any such horses.

4. If no first or second choices qualify, take the third choices of the individual selectors. If there are any that were not named in the consensus, nor picked for first or second by individual selectors, consider any such horses.

5. In case of a tie in which two or more horses must be considered under the conditions given—as very frequently happens—play the horse with the highest tote board odds shortly before post time.

6. In case any choice is scratched, simply disregard it. Consider the remaining horses and pick the one most eligible by the rules.

7. If no horses qualify according to the conditions given, pass up the race entirely. Also pass up any

race where the choice may seem too doubtful, as it is not necessary to play them all.

Here are samples of how the rules would apply with the choices of seven selectors, plus the consensus:

	A	B	C	D	E	F	G	CONSENSUS
SELECTORS' CHOICES RACE X								
1st	Gordo	Teller	Y Gal	Teller	Teller	Teller	Gordo	**Teller**
2nd	Teller	Gordo	Teller	Bully	Bully	Starla	Teller	**Gordo**
3rd	Wilder	Y Gal	Gordo	Gordo	Gordo	Gordo	Bully	**Bully**

In this Race X, the pick was Y Gal. Three horses—Teller, Gordo and Bully—were eliminated as consensus choices. The only lone choice for first was Y Gal. If Y Gal had been scratched, the choice would have been Starla, the only loner given as a second choice. If Starla too had been scratched, the play would have been on Wilder, a lone third.

	A	B	C	D	E	F	G	CONSENSUS
SELECTORS' CHOICES RACE Y								
1st	Drake	Highly	Mr. M	Mine	Drake	Linda	Highly	**Highly**
2nd	Mr. M	Linda	Highly	Linda	Tickle	Sheen	Drake	**Drake**
3rd	Highly	Mr. M	Spider	Drake	Highly	Highly	Mine	**Linda**

The choice in Race Y was between Mr. M. and Mine. At post time, the odds were 12 to 1 on Mine and 10 to 1 on Mr. M., which made Mine the final choice. Linda, listed third in the consensus, could not be considered as a lone first choice.

SELECTORS' CHOICES RACE Z							
	A	**B**	**C**	**D**	**E**	**F**	**G**	**CONSENSUS**
1st	Largo	Largo	Largo	Largo	Largo	Betty	Largo	**Largo**
2nd	Treble	Treble	Piper	Helio	Betty	Largo	Betty	**Betty**
3rd	Helio	Helio	Sinbad	Betty	Sinbad	Waldo	Sinbad	**Treble**

In Race Z, Betty appeared in the consensus, hence was not eligible as a lone first choice. That invoked Rule 3, which made it a tossup, between two lone second choices, Piper and Helio. Piper was scratched, so Helio, at 20 to 1 odds, became the only pick. If Helio had been scratched, Waldo, the only lone third choice, at slightly over 20 to 1, would have rated a play.

Here are the results in a series of thirty races played according to this system. These are given on the basis of a $2 wager, with individual returns on straight, place and show. A few unplayable races occurred, but these are not included in the series.

PLAYING THE LONG SHOTS

	STRAIGHT	PLACE	SHOW	ODDS TO $1
	RESULTS OF 30 RACES			
1	....	....	....	$20.55
2	....	....	....	19.50*
3	...	...	...	4.25
4	$13.90	$7.00	$5.20	5.95
5	...	....	...	5.75
6	....	...	...	10.75
7	....	....	....	6.10
8	...	....	....	17.10*
9	...	...	4.00	3.95
10	....	6.30	3.70	11.65
11	...	...	...	4.25
12	...	10.00	3.70	10.25
13	....	....	....	7.00
14	...	....	....	4.20
15	...	...	3.10	3.20
16	40.40	12.80	5.40	19.20
17	...	....	....	13.40*
18	....	....	....	4.35
19	....	....	....	12.80
20	....	5.10	3.90	4.20
21	....	....	....	3.75
22	...	....	....	24.30*
23	...	....	5.20	9.40
24	31.30	10.80	9.10	14.65*
25	....	....	4.50	18.20
26	16.30	5.10	2.80	7.15
27	...	...	...	5.00
28	5.50	3.70	2.80	1.75
29	....	6.00	4.30	4.85
30	...	...	...	5.75
	$107.40	**$63.80**	**$58.20**	

In the races marked with an asterisk, preference was given to a horse with higher odds. In two races, the un-played horse came home a winner. One paid $7.20 straight, $4.40 place and $3.40 show; the other paid $9.50 straight, $5.50 place and $4.60 show. Playing both horses in such races ensures a winner, when there happens to be one. When playing across the board—straight, place and show—both choices may occasionally pay off. Such a play is advisable when the horse with higher odds is a real long shot, running at 15 to 1 or more.

Similarly, there is no need to play the lower-priced horse once the odds are cut down below a profitable level, say 3 to 1 or lower. The price is right, no matter how low it goes, when that horse is the only choice by this system. But with two horses, the player should make sure that both promise sufficient profit.

The same applies to coupled entries. If a horse that is eligible for play is linked with another, pass it up, unless the odds are reasonably good, say 4 to 1 or better. The main purpose of this system is to get good prices, so an entry must be worthwhile to be playable.

If the race includes a low-priced entry, it is a good idea to pass it up entirely. There is no use in backing a horse that must outrun a pair so good that they are linked to beat the entire field. Similarly, it is unwise to back a horse that is listed with the field, as the odds may be too low in such cases.

In the series listed, only the straight bets were highly profitable, with place and show just about holding their own. That raises the question of how the races should be played. Basically, straight bets are preferable with this system in order to cash in heavily on long shots. However, betting both straight and place may be advisable, as often a chosen horse is only picked to finish second, at best. Show bets are not recommended, as the chance for profit is too slight.

PLAYING THE LONG SHOTS

Here are the totals of some sample series, which include (as Series A) the one just listed, race by race:

RESULTS OF FOUR SAMPLE SERIES							
SERIES	RACES AT $2	BET	STRAIGHT	BET	PLACE	BET	SHOW
A	30	$60	$107.40	$60	$63.80	$60	$58.20
B	35	$70	54.40	$70	55.00	$70	80.40
C	50	$100	90.20	$100	113.60	$100	83.70
D	35	$70	77.10	$70	79.30	$70	78.60
Totals	150	$300	$329.10	$300	$321.70	$300	$300.90

Even with the drop-off in Series B, both straight and place wagers showed overall profits; and the straight deficit in Series C was nullified by the place profit. But the show wagers just about broke even throughout, with little promise of any sizable gains.

By wagering on a $2 straight, $4 place, a player is apt to get more for his $6 than by making a combination bet ($2 each on straight, place and show). In this case, doubling the place bets (and eliminating show) would have netted $52.50 profit, as opposed to $41.40 across the board.

Progressive betting systems are another way of wagering that many horseracing fans enjoy. Several proven progressions are discussed in the next chapter.

10 PROGRESSIVE BETTING SYSTEMS

Many racing fans have gained an introduction to progressive betting with their first $2 bet. They have tempered their disappointment at seeing their horse lose by deciding that the next try may bring better luck. If so, why not make up for the first loss by simply doubling the wager on the second play?

So they do just that and a win nullifies the first loss, while racking up a profit on the new play.

Of course, a second loss leaves just one logical answer: to double up again. So losses of $2 and $4 would mean a wager of $8 on the third race, and another loss would demand a $16 bet on the fourth race, and so on, $32, $64, $128, $256, $512, $1,024, which is a lot of money to put up in order to make good a $2 bet that was a wrong guess in the first place.

That is progression—but not in the right direction. There are, however, modified forms of progressions that offer real potential. Here are four of them.

PROGRESSIVE SYSTEM #1: THE SLOW PROGRESSION

This starts with a basic bet, say $2. If the player wins, he makes the same bet again. If he loses, he bets the amount of his original wager; and if he loses again, he bets the total of his two

previous wagers. He continues in this way after each successive loss, always betting the total of the last two.

Ten consecutive losses would therefore run: 2, 2, 4, 6, 10, 16, 26, 42, 68, and 110. This marks the limit of the series. Note that a first bet of $2 is followed by a bet of $2, as that was the original wager. But the third bet ($6) is composed of the two bets just before it ($2 and $4), and so on.

This progression is geared to odds of 1.60 to 1 or better. Assuming that each winning play hit that amount exactly, the player would break even, or show a slight profit anywhere along the line, as follows:

SLOW PROGRESSION				
LOSSES IN A ROW	**RACE**	**RESULT**	**BET**	**RETURN**
	1	Lose	$2	...
1	2	Win	2	$5.20
		Total	**$4**	**$5.20**
	RACE	**RESULT**	**BET**	**RETURN**
	1	Lose	$2	...
2	2	Lose	2	...
	3	Win	4	$10.40
		Total	**$8**	**$10.40**
	RACE	**RESULT**	**BET**	**RETURN**
	1	Lose	$2	...
	2	Lose	2	...
3	3	Lose	4	...
	4	Win	6	$15.60
		Total	**$14**	**$15.60**
	RACE	**RESULT**	**BET**	**RETURN**
	1	Lose	$2	...
	2	Lose	2	...
	3	Lose	4	...
4	4	Lose	6	...
	5	Win	10	$26.00
		Total	**$24**	**$26.00**
	RACE	**RESULT**	**BET**	**RETURN**
	1	Lose	$2	...
	2	Lose	2	...
	3	Lose	4	...
5	4	Lose	6	...
	5	Lose	10	...
	6	Win	16	$41.60
		Total	**$40**	**$41.60**

Six consecutive losses would require a bet of $26 on the seventh race, making a total of $66 in wagers, bringing a return of $67.60 from a win in the seventh race.

Seven consecutive losses would require a bet of $42 on the eighth race, a total of $108 with a return of $109.20 from a win.

Eight consecutive losses would require a bet of $68 on the ninth race, a total of $176 with a return of $176.80 from a win.

Nine consecutive losses would require a bet of $110 on the tenth race, a total of $286 with a return of $286 from a win.

Ten consecutive losses would result in total loss of $286 for that series. Therein lies the weakness of the progression, and it raises two questions:

1. Can you afford to risk that amount?
2. Is the risk worth the possible return?

If playing favorites at a major track, you are not likely to encounter ten straight losses at the very start. With $286 as starting capital, you have a strong chance of building up a bankroll before that amount is wiped out. As an example: At an Eastern track, more than 200 races were run before Player A encountered ten losses in a row. By then, he was well enough ahead to afford it.

With an initial capital of $572, a player should be fully equipped for the worst, as twenty consecutive losses by favorites is almost unheard of. This means that there should be some profit between two adverse runs of ten straight losses each.

Still, the risk may not be worth it, as it may take too many small wins to compensate for one big loss. One way of meeting that situation is to cut down the length of each series. As an example: A limit of seven consecutive losses would mean a deficit of only $66 for that series. That is not too difficult to regain, provided you do not run into another losing series right away, which is the real danger of this shorter play.

PROGRESSIVE SYSTEM #2: THE STEEP PROGRESSION

Here, working from a basic bet, say $2, the player goes after a quick return, with a profit besides, following a loss, but he quits before he gets in too deep. There are four wagers in each sequence, the initial bet ($2) and three more that are double all the previous totals, making the series simply 2, 4, 12, 36.

After each win, the player begins all over, and if he misses on the whole series, he takes his loss of $54. The progression is steep, as its name implies, but a player can clear it by backing odds-on favorites, which have a fifty-fifty chance of winning at many tracks.

Assuming that the player wins on horses at .50 to 1, which pays $3 on a $2 ticket, he would make out thus:

STEEP PROGRESSION				
LOSSES IN A ROW	**RACE**	**RESULT**	**BET**	**RETURN**
	1	Lose	$2	...
1	2	Win	4	$6.00
		Total	**$6**	**$6.00**
	RACE	**RESULT**	**BET**	**RETURN**
	1	Lose	$2	...
2	2	Lose	4	...
	3	Win	12	$18.00
		Total	**$18**	**$18.00**
	RACE	**RESULT**	**BET**	**RETURN**
	1	Lose	$2	...
	2	Lose	4	...
3	3	Lose	12	...
	4	Win	36	$54.00
		Total	**$54**	**$54.00**

With this steep progression, a few timely hits at fairly good odds will more than make up for some of the wipeouts, particularly when they come on the fourth play of the series. As an example, a win at 2 to 1, paying $6 on a $2 ticket, would bring in $108, clearing not only that sequence but another losing series as well.

PROGRESSIVE SYSTEM #3: THE PERCENTAGE PROGRESSION

This system is a safeguard against heavy loss. It starts with a fixed sum, say $10, and calls for a minimum wager of 20 percent of that amount, $2 in this case. If the original sum is used up, the player starts over with the same amount ($10). However, when the fund reaches a higher level, in this instance $20, the player increases his bet accordingly. Thus with a bankroll of $20, a 20 percent wager would be $4. Upon reaching the $30 level, it would be $6, and so on. At some fixed level, say $50 or above, the profit can be laid aside and a new start made with a $10 fund.

This can be done on an approximate basis, as a few dollars one way or the other makes little difference. The important point is that the percentage increases as the player wins and decreases as he loses, so that once he is ahead, he is working in a sense with the track's money, not his own. If his original $10 fund drops to nothing, he starts over with a new $10 investment.

The chart on page page 141 shows how these progressions work out in comparison with flat bets of a fixed amount over a series of 24 races at a well-known track.

PROGRESSION CHART

RACE	FLAT BETS ($2) BET	STR.	PLACE	SHOW	SLOW PROGRESS BET	RETURN	STEEP PROGRESS BET	RETURN	PERCENTAGE BET	RETURN	FUND $10
1	$2	$6.10	$4.90	$3.20	$2	$6.10	$2	$6.10	$2	$6.10	$14.10
2	2	...	...	...	2	...	2	...	2	...	12.10
3	2	...	2.50	2.20	2	...	4	...	2	...	10.10
4	2	5.20	3.10	2.40	4	10.40	12	31.20	2	5.20	13.30
5	2	...	...	...	2	...	2	...	2	...	11.30
6	2	...	2.20	2.10	2	...	4	...	2	...	9.30
7	2	3.50	3.00	2.40	4	7.00	12	21.00	2	3.50	10.80
8	2	...	...	...	2	...	2	...	2	...	8.80
9	2	6.60	4.20	3.50	2	6.60	4	13.20	2	6.60	13.40
10	2	...	...	...	2	...	2	...	2	...	11.40
11	2	6.60	4.00	2.90	2	6.60	4	13.20	2	6.60	16.00
12	2	...	...	...	2	...	2	...	2	...	14.00
13	2	4.40	2.60	2.20	2.	4.40	4	8.80	2	4.40	16.40
14	2	...	...	...	2.	...	2	...	2	...	14.40
15	2	6.00	3.70	2.50	2	6.00	4	12.00	2	6.00	18.40
16	2	6.10	3.90	3.00	2	6.10	2	6.10	4	12.20	26.60
17	2	6.10	3.70	2.60	2	6.10	2	6.10	4	12.20	34.80
18	2	...	...	...	2	...	2	...	6	...	28.80
19	2	5.30	3.70	3.30	2	5.30	4	10.60	6	15.90	38.70
20	2	...	...	...	2	...	2	...	8	...	30.70
21	2	6.50	3.10	2.20	2	6.50	4	13.00	6	19.50	44.20
22	2	...	...	...	2	...	2	...	8	...	36.20
23	2	4.70	3.10	2.60	2	4.70	4	9.40	6	14.10	44.30
24	2	4.50	3.50	2.80	2	4.50	2	4.50	8	18.00	54.30
	$48	$71.60	$51.20	$39.90	$52	$80.30	$86	$155.20	$86	Fund	$54.30
	Less 48.00	48.00	48.00	48.00	Profit 52.00	52.00	Profit 86.00	86.00		Less	10.00
	Profit	$23.60	$3.20	-$8.10		$28.30		$69.20		Profit	$44.30

PROGRESSIVE SYSTEM #4:
THE STEADY INVESTMENT PLAN

Here is a way of staggering wagers with low odds so that between them, they promise a constant profit. The player collects much more often than he loses and this frequency factor is helpful to his confidence as well as his exchequer. But it is unwise to get overconfident or to expect too much return from what is primarily a form of safety play. What is more, the safety factor also bears close watching.

Although this is a conservative system, any type of race is played. Maidens and two-year-olds are especially welcome, as will become apparent. However, a sufficient bankroll is required to gain worthwhile results, otherwise you won't make enough profit to get back your admission money at the track. Therefore, this system is not for the $2 bettor. A $20 play per race is more like it.

That in turn would mean available capital of close to $500, though often the system begins to build from the very start, providing the player with the very reserve funds that he may need later. So it is described here on the basis of a $20 play, though anyone is quite welcome to try it on a $5 or even a $2 plan, where it may serve as a supplement to some more spectacular type of play.

First, note the wagering method, as it is the keynote of the system. Starting with $20 on the first horse, the player bets that basic sum in every succeeding race. Each time he loses, he must add $40 to the next play. Thus, if he started with four losers in a row, his wagers would run $20, $60, $100, and $140, making a loss of $320 with the racing day only half gone.

That's not a way to make money—it is a way to lose it. But such an opening is seldom encountered, as the horses are picked on the most conservative basis; namely, in each race, the player takes the horse with the lowest odds and bets it to show.

The only exception is when the horse proves to be an odds-on favorite; then the player bets it to place.

About 35 percent of favorites prove to be winners and that figure is usually more than doubled where finishing in the money is concerned. The player thus is backing horses that may have a 75 percent chance of paying off, though on a very trifling scale.

However, when a horse does pay off, the player automatically reduces his wager by $20. Thus if it finishes in the money on a $100 bet, the next play would be for $80. If that horse comes through, the next play would be $60, and so forth down the line.

Simple arithmetic reveals that if two-thirds of the favorites merely show, the bets will be dropping down as fast as they go up. So the player will gradually get it down to the $20 minimum, which completes the series. Another is begun with $20, and each time such a wager comes through, the player pockets it and begins anew.

The races listed on the next page illustrate this system. They were held at a major track, and each starred amount represents a new start, bringing a total profit of $243. Reduced to the proportions of a $2 bet, this would only bring a profit of $46.30 over a six-day period, which is not enough for the expense and time involved. Hence the necessity for the $20 play, though, as mentioned before, you may pick a level in between.

Flat bets of $10 would result in a $231 profit, requiring a much smaller bankroll or reserve fund at the outset of the play.

RESULTS OF 48 RACES USING STEADY INVESTMENT PLAN

RACE	AMOUNT	RETURN	RACE	AMOUNT	RETURN
1	$20*	$0	26	20*	26
2	60	63	27	20*	27
3	40	50	28	20*	38
4	20*	0	29	20*	0
5	60	78	30	60	90
6	40	0	31	40	0
7	80	0	32	80	104
8	120	228	33	60	93
9	100	150	34	40	54
10	80	118	35	20*	0
11	60	0	36	60	0
12	100	170	37	100	140
13	80	92	38	80	108
14	60	0	39	60	71
15	100	145	40	40	56
16	80	128	41	20*	0
17	60	114	42	60	84
18	40	50	43	40	74
19	20*	0	44	20*	0
20	60	0	45	60	84
21	100	140	46	40	52
22	80	108	47	20*	29
23	60	84	48	20*	31
24	40	62		$2580	$2954
25	20*	33	Profit:	$374	

11 THE DAILY DOUBLE

This is an outgrowth of a type of betting known as a two-horse parlay, in which a player puts a wager on a horse with the understanding that if he wins, the entire amount, including the original stake, is to go on another horse in a later race, whatever the odds may be. Both horses, of course, are named prior to the first race; otherwise, there would be no parlay.

A two-horse parlay may be modified so that the player takes out the original investment (if he wins the first race) and simply puts the balance on the next nag. In any case, a parlay attracts many players, because it gives them the false thrill of thinking that they are playing with the track's money, which they aren't. Once a bundle of cash is in a player's pocket, it is his own and doesn't belong to anybody else.

With a true parlay, however, there is no pulling out. This concept applies to the daily double. In the **daily double**, the player must pick a combination of two horses, each from a different race—usually the first and second races—that are specified by the track. In order to collect, his horses must win both races. It isn't a case of letting the first horse's winnings ride along with the second, either in whole or in part. The parlay is a single transaction throughout.

PROS AND CONS OF BETTING THE DAILY DOUBLE

Since the daily double is a single transaction, many players like it. Only one deduction of 15 percent is taken instead of two, because the bets go into a special daily-double pool. Further, the pay-off odds are determined by the amount of money in that pool and not by the regular betting on the races in question. Since smart bettors seldom wager heavily on the daily double, this frequently produces freakish odds that are to the average player's advantage.

Added up, this means that the winner of a daily double usually fares better—and sometimes much better—than if he had played the same two races as a regular two-horse parlay.

On the other side of the ledger, the player has no choice of races as he would with a two-horse parlay. At some tracks, one or both of the races slated for the daily double are run by untried horses, the types of races that most astute players would pass up, making them all the harder to predict. Also, a large number of horses often are entered in such events, which adds to the difficulty. As one disillusioned racing fan phrased it: "When I started playing daily doubles, I thought I was backing horses, but when I finished, I realized I'd been picking dogs."

MINIMIZING LOSSES

However, there are ways of playing daily doubles and cushioning the losses. The one sure method of getting some money back is to put a $2 bet on every possible combination of horses in the two races forming the daily double. That means that the player is sure to cash in on a winning ticket, but he is not likely to show a profit.

With a dozen horses in each race, the cost for such a round robin would be $288. While pay-offs on a daily double occasionally exceed that amount and may even go much higher, there are many that fall far short.

It is like playing long shots but on a grander scale, with a player hoping that one big win will put him so far ahead that he can quit right then. But if it doesn't hit soon enough, he will be digging out of a hole that keeps getting deeper.

Take this series of daily-double pay-offs over a four-week period at a major track, with ten to twelve horses in each race, requiring an average play of $200 to $288 for each daily double:

DAILY DOUBLE PAYOFFS OVER FOUR WEEKS							
	PAYOFF		PAYOFF		PAYOFF		PAYOFF
1	$154.80	7	$20.10	13	$561.30	19	$95.60
2	495.10	8	56.00	14	136.10	20	115.90
3	40.80	9	45.90	15	19.00	21	67.00
4	75.00	10	387.80	16	89.60	22	23.10
5	19.30	11	159.70	17	66.90	23	14.90
6	49.70	12	75.30	18	48.20	24	45.30

While this showed a profit after the second day, from then on it declined, so that by the completion of the series, an investment of close to $6,000 brought a return of $2,862.40.

Since money obviously can't be made that way, the first step to sanity is to cut down on the total of combination plays by eliminating some of the least likely nags, even if it does blow any chance for a super-duper payoff.

DAILY DOUBLE SYSTEM #1: SIMPLE DAILY DOUBLE SYSTEM

This is perhaps the simplest of daily-double systems and one that has been used continually by many players. You pick a horse in the first race and combine it with every horse in the

second race, buying a $2 ticket on each combo. Thus, if you back the favorite in the first race and there are twelve horses running in the second race, the play will cost you exactly $24. If your horse wins in the first race, you are sure to cash a winning ticket on the daily double, the size of the return hinging upon which horse wins the second race.

Basically, this system of play is no tougher—and no easier—than picking a winner in a single race, because it amounts to just that and nothing more. It simply brings the "double" down to a "single," but with one interesting difference, as follows.

If you feel that your horse is worth backing to the extent of $24, you could—and probably would—put that amount on the horse to win, playing the nag on that race only. That, in fact, would have to be your procedure under ordinary circumstances. But when the daily double is involved, you have this option of playing "one for all" in the manner just described.

The question is: Will you make out better?

Where the play of a favorite or low-odds horse is concerned, you have strong possibilities of increasing your return, as will be seen from the sample charts that follow. These show the results of a series of twelve races at a major track, according to stated patterns of play.

RESULTS OF DAILY DOUBLE IN 12 RACES

DAILY DOUBLE	# IN 2ND RACE	A COST	A RETURN	B COST	B RETURN	# IN 1ST RACE	C COST	C RETURN	D COST	D RETURN
1	12	24	$86.20	24	⋮	12	24	⋮	24	⋮
2	12	24	⋮	24	⋮	12	24	$273.40	24	⋮
3	10	20	⋮	20	$69.40	9	18	⋮	18	⋮
4	12	24	22.00	24	⋮	12	24	22.00	24	⋮
5	12	24	⋮	24	⋮	12	24	87.80	24	⋮
6	10	20	⋮	20	⋮	12	24	⋮	24	$161.80
7	12	24	⋮	24	⋮	12	24	⋮	24	⋮
8	12	24	⋮	24	⋮	11	22	130.20	22	⋮
9	12	24	⋮	24	⋮	12	24	⋮	24	⋮
10	12	24	⋮	24	⋮	12	24	⋮	24	93.40
11	11	22	56.80	22	⋮	12	24	⋮	24	56.80
12	12	24	⋮	24	30.40	12	24	⋮	24	30.40
		$278	$165	$278	$99.80		$280	$513.40	$280	$342.40

Key to the Chart
A: First-race favorite and all second-race horses
B: First-race contender and all second-race horses
C: Second-race favorite and all first-race horses
D: Second-race contender and all first-race horses

From this instance, we find that backing the first-race favorite as the pivot in a daily double brought a deficit of $113.80. Anyone who backed the first-race contender or the second-best choice on the same basis fared even worse, losing $128.20, which is a lot for two weeks of effort.

However, backing the second-race favorite in the same manner proved a profitable venture, putting the player $233.40 to the good. A play on the second-race contender was also worthwhile: It netted $62.40, but the wins came late in the series. Only when backing the second-race favorite as the key horse did the player put himself far ahead to stay.

Now, suppose that the player had backed each horse to win its own race, disregarding the other half of the daily double, but putting the full amount of the wager on that horse alone. Here is how the results would have compared:

BACKING EACH HORSE TO WIN

A FAVORITES IN FIRST RACES

DAY OF WIN	RETURN ON $2 TICKET	AMOUNT OF WAGER	RETURN STRAIGHT BET	DAILY DOUBLE RETURN
1	$6.40	$24	$76.80	$86.20
4	9.00	24	108.00	22.00
11	5.20	22	57.20	56.80
			$242.00	**$165.00**

B CONTENDERS IN FIRST RACES

DAY OF WIN	RETURN ON $2 TICKET	AMOUNT OF WAGER	RETURN STRAIGHT BET	DAILY DOUBLE RETURN
3	$9.40	$20	$94.00	$69.40
12	10.20	24	122.40	30.40
			$216.40	**$99.80**

C FAVORITES IN SECOND RACE

DAY OF WIN	RETURN ON $2 TICKET	AMOUNT OF WAGER	RETURN STRAIGHT BET	DAILY DOUBLE RETURN
2	$7.00	$24	$84.00	$273.40
4	4.80	24	57.60	22.00
5	8.30	24	105.60	87.80
8	4.60	22	50.60	130.20
			$297.80	**$513.40**

D CONTENDERS IN SECOND RACE

DAY OF WIN	RETURN ON $2 TICKET	AMOUNT OF WAGER	RETURN STRAIGHT BET	DAILY DOUBLE RETURN
6	$8.20	$24	$98.40	$161.80
10	9.40	24	112.80	93.40
11	7.00	24	84.00	56.80
12	9.00	24	108.00	30.40
			$403.20	**$342.40**

All this breaks down as follows:

A: Backing 1st-race favorite and all 2nd-race horses in combination:
Loss $113.80
Backing favorite alone:
Loss $36.00

B: Backing 1st-race contender and all 2nd-race horses in combination:
Loss $128.20
Backing contender alone:
Loss $61.60

C: Backing 2nd-race favorite and all 1st-race horses in combination:
Gain $233.40
Backing favorite alone:
Gain $17.80

D: Backing 2nd-race contender and all 1st-race horses in combination:
Gain $62.40
Backing contender alone:
Gain $123.20

The "big win" goes to the daily double, by virtue of one large payoff on the second day, when backing the favorite in the second race in combination with all the first-race horses (Chart C). Otherwise, a straight play on the key horse alone was a better bet than the daily double.

Naturally, these few figures do not tell the full story, but they indicate clearly that the daily double depends upon lucky breaks or freakish combinations to bring good results. Otherwise, it loses more than a normal wager should.

DAILY DOUBLE SYSTEM #2: ELIMINATING UNLIKELY LONG SHOTS

Obviously, if a player put only $12 instead of $28 on his key horse, the daily double would be more profitable proportionately, and thereby would be a better bet than playing that horse alone. Some players handle this by eliminating the most unlikely long shots from their combination.

For example, on the first day listed, the first race had four horses running at odds of 48 to 1, 60 to 1, 77 to 1, and 96 to 1, respectively. By eliminating those, a player would have saved $8 right there, and further pruning would have cut down the investment still more. But in so doing, he would have jeopardized his key horse bet in the second race. If one of those long shots did come through, his whole bet would be lost.

Another problem with the daily double is this: It is difficult to pick the first-race favorite or the next best horse as contender because the windows close early on the daily double. This makes the odds unreliable, because there may be sharp changes on the tote board before race time. Though the daily double is a separate pool, the odds in the first race are the player's index to the desired key horse.

If he is using a key horse from the second race, the player's choice must be sheer guesswork, because he has to buy his daily-double ticket before the first race, so he never gets a glimpse of the tote board in the second race. Some of the supposed long shots that a player eliminates may turn out to be low-priced runners by the time the horses are at the post.

Most daily-double betting is therefore done on the strength of the morning line, or according to the choices of good selectors. There is nothing bad about that, as some players operate on such a basis continually. When the selectors agree on a favorite, the tote board is apt to register the same.

Here is how a daily double can, and did, click when played in that fashion:

a. In the first race, the selectors were divided in their choice of a favorite, with seven horses in the race.

b. In the second race, the selectors were unanimous in their choice of a favorite, with eight horses in the race.

So, the player took the favorite in the second race as a "sure" post-time favorite. He used it as the key horse and bought seven tickets, coupling the second-race favorite with each of the first-race horses. The consensus choice for the first race remained the favorite at post time, but two other horses were backed heavily and another pair were given a healthy play, so that the last two nags in the betting were running at odds of 31 to 1 and 43 to 1, respectively. As luck had it, the 43 to 1 shot came through.

In the second race, the selected favorite became the post-time favorite at less than 2 to 1, with most of the rest running at much higher odds. In this race, the favorite came through. Therefore, the daily double paid off on the "worst" horse in the first race and the "best" horse in the second race to the tune of $387.60 on a $2 ticket, a nice harvest for the player who invested $14.

The horse that won the first race paid $89.70 on a $2 straight ticket, so if it had been backed with the full $14, it would have brought home $627.90. But no player in his right mind would have backed such a long shot, which had won only one race in its last twenty-two starts. But as simply one of the combination bets, the $2 put on the long shot brought in $387.60, or more than four times the amount offered by a $2 straight bet.

In contrast, if the player had put his $14 on the favorite in the second race as a straight bet, its pay off of $5.70 on a $2 ticket would only have been $39.90. So that amount, $39.90, was stepped up to nearly ten times its normal payoff. Therefore, the daily double proved a good bet, amounting in substance to a sound play on the second-race favorite, with an outright gamble on the first race, but a gamble in which the player had more to gain than lose.

BIZARRE DAILY DOUBLE SYSTEMS

Some daily-double systems are really on the bizarre side. For example, one method calls for covering all horses in the first race with varying amounts according to their probable odds, putting as high as $10 on a 2 to 1 horse and as little as $2 on those in the long-shot category. Then, of course, all are combined with a likely winner in the second race. But here again, the player is apt to be defeating himself. Giving the long shots less play is safer than eliminating them, but there is a waste of capital on those lower priced nags which so often bring a disappointing payoff in a daily double.

Also, there is the difficulty of rating them properly, where odds are concerned. If you are really after something more solid in the daily double, you should delve into System #3 discussed below.

DAILY DOUBLE SYSTEM #3: THE CRISSCROSS SYSTEM

This is an effort to equalize the two races of the daily double by picking a winner from each. It assumes that none of the horses in either event are too solid or those races would not have been slated for the daily double.

That makes it very simple. You study the selections in your favorite newspaper or racing journal and back the top three choices in each half of the daily double. For convenience, we

will label those of the first race as A, B and C; those in the second race as X, Y and Z. These horses are the consensus selections, so that if any are scratched, you can promote the next-best choice to the favored top three.

The normal cost of backing these steeds as daily doublers is $18 on the following basis:

A with X $2	B with X $2	C with X $2
A with Y $2	B with Y $2	C with Y $2
A with Z $2	B with Z $2	C with Z $2

Taking it from there, let's look at a sample week.

THE DAILY DOUBLE

CRISSCROSS SYSTEM WEEK 1

MONDAY

FIRST RACE		SECOND RACE	
	A finished 10th		X finished 2nd
	B finished 4th		Y finished 3rd
	C finished 3rd		Z finished 1st

Nice, particularly the second race, except that each event should have shown a winner, which is necessary in this system. So the player lost $18 on Monday.

TUESDAY

FIRST RACE		SECOND RACE	
	A finished 1st		X finished 10th
	B finished 3rd		Y finished 3rd
	C finished 10th		Z finished 7th

Again, the double did not link. Another loss of $18.

WEDNESDAY

FIRST RACE		SECOND RACE	
	A finished 3rd		X finished 3rd
	B finished 8th		Y finished 2nd
	C finished 6th		Z finished 1st

They missed in the first, but ran close to form in the second race. Again, a loss of $18.

THURSDAY

FIRST RACE		SECOND RACE	
	A finished 1st*		X finished 6th
	B finished 2nd*		Y finished 2nd
	C finished 11th		Z finished 4th

In the first race, the two top choices finished in a dead heat so that both participated in the daily double, but the system player didn't because he missed a winner in the second race.

FRIDAY

FIRST RACE		SECOND RACE	
	A finished 5th		X finished 2nd
	B finished 1st		Y finished 7th
	C finished 6th		Z finished 1st

Another $18 invested for a total of $90 and this time a payoff (on B and Z) that came to $80.60. This represented a loss of $9.40 for the five-day play, but it illustrates how one good win can offset previous losses. Now let's look at another week:

CRISSCROSS SYSTEM WEEK 2			
MONDAY			
FIRST RACE	A finished 2nd	**SECOND RACE**	X finished 4th
	B finished 4th		Y finished 2nd
	C finished 5th		Z finished 3rd
TUESDAY			
FIRST RACE	A finished 7th	**SECOND RACE**	X finished 1st
	B finished 4th		Y finished 5th
	C finished 8th		Z finished 3rd
WEDNESDAY			
FIRST RACE	A finished 6th	**SECOND RACE**	X finished 1st
	B finished 1st		Y finished 2nd
	C finished 8th		Z finished 7th
Daily double payoff (on B and X): $23.50.			
THURSDAY			
FIRST RACE	A finished 7th	**SECOND RACE**	X finished 1st
	B finished 1st		Y finished 2nd
	C finished 3rd		Z finished 5th
Daily double payoff (on B and X): $23.20.			
FRIDAY			
FIRST RACE	A finished 1st	**SECOND RACE**	X finished 2nd
	B finished 7th		Y finished 3rd
	C finished 11th		Z finished 1st
Daily double payoff (on A and Z): $32.10.			

Compare this daily double payoff with the previous week. Again, a daily investment of $18 totaled an outlay of $90. In this case, the return came to $78.80, which represented a loss of $11.20, although the daily double hit on three days out of five. Here, the ratio between investment and return is the problem.

One method of tightening play is to back only the top two choices in each race in crisscross combination, thus playing A with X, A with Y, B with X, and B with Y for a total cost of only $8 a day.

THE DAILY DOUBLE

In the first week shown, that required $40 and the whole outlay was a loss, since none of those combos clicked. In the second week, another play of $40 brought $43.70, which was a mere $3.70 profit. Such results stress the complaint of many players: when they do win on the top-two combo, the payoffs are too small. Hence many players prefer straight bets on the daily double, a single horse from each race, backed by a $2 ticket or multiple thereof. An extended survey of such results indicates that combining the favorites as picked by selectors (namely, horses A and X) is not generally profitable, as too many other players are apt to pick that same "sure" bet.

Combining the favorite in the first race (A) with the contender in the second race (Y) is preferred by some players, as it promises a better payoff than the A and X setup. In the ten races listed, this A and Y combination would have cost the player $20 (at $2 per race) bringing a round 0 (zero) in return.

In contrast, the reverse combination of first-race contender (B) and second-race favorite (X) was a money doubler. The B and X play cost $20 and brought in $46.70.

Some players have been known to cover both these combinations—A and Y, plus B and X—at the low cost of $4 (a $2 ticket on each combo), thus backing the favorite in each race, but avoiding both together. As a $2 bet, a combination of B and Y is popular, because in many cases these two contenders may be regarded as almost equal to the favorites, yet are not apt to be as heavily played in the daily double. This fluked, however, in the ten races cited.

Similarly, a combination of B and Z (second-best horse with third-best), or a combination of C and Y (third-best with second-best) has certain merit. In the races listed, a play of B and Z would have cost $20 and its one win paid off $80.60 for a profit of $60.60, enough to keep the player in business for the next five weeks with the same B and Z deal. However, a play of C and Y would have left him $20 out and still hoping for a win to bring him back.

> To summarize, before playing daily doubles at a given track, results should be studied in terms of:
> - Caliber of Races
> - Reliability of Selectors
> - Public Betting Trends

Thus one horse in a "sure" race can be combined with all the horses in a "wild" race, *provided* the selectors have been solid in their "sure" choices and that the public has not been combining such horses below the profit margin.

Or, if the two races stack up about the same—say both are fairly "sure" or both fairly "wild"—the crisscross system can be used, again according to selectors' calls and public betting trends.

In all instances, the choices of a single selector may prove better than the consensus, as some come up with fairly frequent winners that are ignored by the rest of the clan. This too should be studied in reference to daily doubles.

This concludes our examination and discussion of horserace betting systems that may or may not lead you to the pay window on your next day at the races.

C CONCLUDING REMARKS: BEING A WINNER

Whether you're new to betting the ponies or an old pro who's been at it for years, the formulas for betting different types of races presented in this book should give you an edge over other bettors. With these methods and systems at your fingertips—and a modicum of study and determination—you will find yourself making the best picks in the right races at the best odds possible.

By now, you know how to evaluate the weight factor and judge the proficiency of the jockey as well as how to use various progressive betting systems. Whether you bet on a horse with only middle odds, wager on a decided long shot, or put your money on the consensus favorite, you can use the multiple methods we've learned here to your advantage in making the best selections.

It is my hope that you will become a consistently successful player at the track, and will walk away from the cashier's window with far more wins than you've ever had before. With some simple number crunching and a desire to become an increasingly more successful handicapper, I am confident you will achieve your goal of beating the races.

 **GLOSSARY**

Across the Board
> A bet on a horse to win, place and show. In racing parlance, a player who buys a combination ticket is betting across the board.

Allowance Race
> A reduction in weight that a horse carries based on certain race conditions, such as the amount of money a horse has won over a certain period, an apprentice jockey, or a female mount racing against males.

Claiming Race
> A race in which every horse is put up for sale and may be claimed at the established price by any bona fide buyer.

Cup Race
> A race that is run by three-year-olds and up.

Daily Double
> A betting option offered by the track in which a bettor must pick the winner for each of two specified races in order to cash his ticket. The Daily Double has its own pari-mutuel pool.

Derby
> A type of stakes race run by three-year-old horses.

Favorite
> The horse that is quoted at the lowest odds.

Field

All the horses running in a race.

Flat Bet

A betting system in which the same amount is played on each race.

Form

The performance records of a horse and his expected current performance. Also, an abbreviation for the *Daily Racing Form*.

Futurity

A stakes race run by horses that were still unborn when they were entered.

Handicap Race

A type of sweepstakes race in which a track handicapper assigns weights to all the horses in the field in order to equalize their speed and produce a close finish.

Handle

Short for **pari-mutuel handle**, a race's handle is the amount of money bettors have wagered on that race.

"If" Bet

A type of betting system wherein, when a player loses a race, he stakes a specified sum on another horse in an effort to recoup.

"In-Betweeners"

Bettors who make place bets.

In the Money

Horses that finish first, second or third are said to be "in the money," since a wager on them returns money to the bettor.

Long Shots

A horse that appears to have only a slim chance of winning, and will return high odds if he does.

GLOSSARY

Maiden Races
Races run by horses that have never won a race. The term "maiden" applies to either sex.

Maturity
A race that is open to four-year-olds only.

Middle Odds
Odds that are above 2 to 1 (the favorite) and below 6 to 1 (the long shot).

Minus Pool
A minus pool is created when a favorite is bet down so low that it pays only $2.10 on a $2 ticket, in which case the track foregoes its 15 percent vigorish.

Morning Line
The odds quoted before wagering begins.

Odds
The chances that a horse will win, from a sportsbook or bookmaker's point of view, adjusted to include a profit.

Odds-on Horse
A horse that runs at less than even money, paying under a dollar for each dollar invested.

On the Nose
A bet placed on a horse to win.

Overlay
A horse whose odds of winning are high when compared with its winning chances.

Parlay
A betting system wherein a player lets his winnings from one race carry over to the next.

Past Performance Chart
A condensation of results charts, usually published in racing forms, covering a horse's performances over as many as a dozen races.

Pick Six

A betting option offered by the track in which a bettor picks a winner for each of six specified races. Like the Daily Double, the Pick Six has its own pari-mutuel pool.

Place Bet

A bet that a horse will finish in first or second place.

Plater

A horse that habitually runs in claiming races.

Progression Betting

A type of wagering that calls for regular increases of bets on certain races, as opposed to always making flat bets.

Quinella

A form of betting two horses to place in the same specified race, with both needing to finish in one-two order for the bettor to win.

Scratched

A horse that was scheduled to run in a race but did not.

Second Favorite

A handicapper's second choice to win a race.

Show Bet

A wager that a horse will finish first, second, or third in a race.

Steep Progression

A type of betting system that greatly increases wagers after lost bets.

Steeplechase Races

A type of race in which the participating horses, often called "jumpers," must clear hedges and ditches.

Straight

A wager placed on a horse to win.

Sweepstakes or stakes races

Races in which the stakes are posted by the owners, with the prizes split by the top four winners.

Totalizator

An electronic device that tabulates the bets and flashes the numbers of the horses, along with their odds, on a huge bulletin board called the **tote board.**

Underlay

A horse whose tote board odds drop below a well-estimated figure.

Win Bet

A synonym for "straight bet"—a bet on a horse to win.

Workout

A timed training run that a horse runs prior to a race, the results of which are published in the *Daily Racing Form.*